The Faith

of the Church

THE FAITH

OF THE CHURCH

*A commentary on
the Apostle's Creed
according to
Calvin's Catechism*

By KARL BARTH

Edited by JEAN-LOUIS LEUBA

Translated by GABRIEL VAHANIAN

LIVING AGE BOOKS

published by MERIDIAN BOOKS, INC. New York

Karl Barth

Karl Barth, it is unnecessary to observe, is one of the major theologians of the twentieth century. Beginning with his crucial work, *Der Roemerbrief* in 1919 (translated under the title, *Epistle to the Romans*) Barth continued to develop in power, trenchancy, and scope of concern. Dr. Gabriel Vahanian, who translated this work from the French, has provided an illuminating introduction as well as one of the most thorough bibliographies of Barth's writings to have been published.

Translated from the French La Confession de Foi de l'Eglise *by Gabriel Vahanian, Department of Religion, Princeton University*

A Living Age Books Original Edition
First published by Living Age Books October 1958
First printing September 1958

© *Copyright by Meridian Books, Inc. 1958*

Library of Congress Catalog Card Number: 58-11930

Manufactured in the United States of America

CONTENTS

INTRODUCTION *by Gabriel Vahanian*

Seldom has Barth been so close to Calvin, and Calvin so close to us, as in the present work, now translated and published in English for the first time. Of course, it is not surprising that Barth should echo Calvin; or that he chose as the framework of his lectures delivered before an audience of Swiss *reformed* • ministers, to use Calvin's *Catechism of the Church of Geneva* of 1545. Everyone acknowledges that Barth has been the leader of the so-called revival *of the spirit* of Reformation

---

• The continental Reformation was composed of two major strands: *Lutheran* (stemming from Luther's initial stand) and *Reformed* (born of the teachings of Calvin and Zwingli), which are to be distinguished from the *Sectarian* movements (Anabaptists, etc.).

7

theology in the present day, and that this means for him primarily reformed theology.

What perhaps is surprising is that never has Calvin himself so compelled us to tread other paths than his own as when he is heard through Barth's interpretation. It will be seen that, for the sake of an equal and common fidelity to the living reality of God, Barth can be marvelously free from Calvin. He can reject him without any feeling of disobedience. But he can also uphold him without reservation. Unlike lesser minds today, he does not have to make Calvin a "Barthian" in order to believe what he says. Nor must he always find some oblique reason in Calvin himself for departing from him in order to write theology in a manner that is truly faithful to the intentions and structure of the rediscovery of the gospel that took place in the period of the Reformation.

The significant characteristic of Barth's approach, however, is that its concern is not at all merely to reveal to us where Calvin was right and where he was wrong; but it reveals to us, through the reformer's teaching, the truth exhibited by the Person, the Word and Work, i.e., by the whole event of Jesus the Christ. This common allegiance, and this alone, accounts for the degree of subjection of Barth's thought to that of Calvin, and at the same time his extraordinary freedom to disagree where he must. This living reality of the Christ-event neither Calvin nor Barth intend to incarcerate in a theological system, as if neatly to conserve the faith forever. Barth's approach reveals to us that the purpose of Calvin's teaching is to let its eternal subject, i.e., the Word become flesh, confront the individual, and perchance the disciple, ever anew.

What this means is that a reformed theologian never writes for posterity. He exhibits the living Word today. Only in this manner can what he has to say to his contemporaries have any relevance for their descendants. He is not a master or a doctor as are Augustine and Thomas Aquinas in the Roman Catholic Church. The reformed theologian is at his best when he strives after the description which Barth, in another context, applied to the author of the *Institutes* "Calvin est pour nous un maître dans l'art d'écouter." • Calvin teaches us how to listen to the Word of God proclaimed, not to himself, but in the Church.

The foregoing should make evident that it is peculiar good fortune—shall we say, providence?— that this book combines Barth's commentary, Calvin's commentary, and the Apostles' Creed. The Creed, or the truth to which the Creed as a symbol refers, is what binds them together.•• Aside from

----

• *Calvin: Textes Choisis,* by Ch. Gagnebin. Preface by K. Barth, p. 10.

••Other works of Karl Barth's in English are, it is true, similar to this book with regard to their aim, *viz.* to discuss some Reformation creedal formulations. His Gifford Lectures, published under the title *The Knowledge of God and the Service of God,* have, however, the disadvantage of being based on the Scottish Confession of 1560, which to say the least is not familiar to the ordinary reader, or even to the theological student. *Dogmatics in Outline,* which comes closest to this, *Prayer,* and, now in paper covers *The Word of God and the Word of Man* will certainly introduce the reader to Barth's thought. Yet the present work is in our estimation perhaps the best simplified and systematic introduction to the theology of Karl Barth in its

being well-known, the preeminence of the Apostles' Creed as the most universally accepted statement of the Christian faith in all ages suggests that what Calvin and Barth individually say about it, and what Barth says about Calvin's commentary upon it, needs careful consideration. This volume may therefore serve many readers as the most readily available introduction to the thought of Karl Barth, and to the Reformation's rediscovery both of the gospel and of the "Catholic" faith enshrined in the Creed.

Barth's theology is in fact contained in the liminal statements of Calvin's catechism. It is no exaggeration to say that there is a similarity between the inner structure of Barth's thought and that of Calvin, for both are related to the Creed. As a matter of fact, it would be wrong to expect less than this, since Barth's systematic theology, like the Creed, consists chiefly in Christological concentration. For this reason, the first article of the Creed (on God as Creator) and the third (on the Holy Spirit and the Church) as well as the second (on the Son) are all interpreted in the sense of God's work of reconciliation, of which the Christ-event (i.e. the love of God for man) constitutes the cornerstone. On this point, Barth finds himself in agreement with Calvin, who "clearly indicates the origin of our knowledge of God's love. Note well: it is not a question of a general and abstract and philosophical knowledge, not a question of a treatise on the love of God in nature or

---

correlation with the Reformation. This is because he is commenting both on the Creed and on Calvin's commentary. See Bibliography.

on love in general; all this, all these abstract ideas are a piece of paper, a great noise, only ideas. The Gospel, on the contrary, tells us about realities. The task of theological reflection and of preaching does not begin at all with abstract ideas, but with the reality of God's action. The love of God is not an abstract quality of God's; it is an act: God takes to heart our misery. In Jesus Christ, he declares his mercy unto us and puts this mercy to work, and there is no mercy towards us outside Jesus Christ."

To be sure, it is not our intention to suggest only how wonderful a coincidence there is in this case between the Reformer's and Barth's views. Actually, more than once Barth will have to part company; for example, on the issue of predestination and the resurrection of the flesh. But what is more interesting is the way in which certain doctrines, under Barth's analysis of Calvin's statements, yield a fresher meaning, sometimes fully daring, sometimes vigorously paradoxical. The reader has but to be referred to the passage where Barth interprets the doctrine of the ascension as implying the ultimate refutation of all dictatorships, or where his understanding of the virgin birth or the empty tomb is both in strict conformity with orthodoxy and—we must admit—wholly unorthodox.

Doubtless some readers may need help in understanding what they will find in this volume. In a brief introduction only a few points can, in any case, be selected for comment. Three points in particular seem to the translator to require further discussion; and they are chosen because they will help to show the originality of Barth's thought by setting this volume in a larger framework and, generally, in relation to his unique contribution to systematic theology as a whole. These points are: (1) theology as corrective and world-facing and, by implication, man-honoring; (2) theology and ethics; and (3) Barth's unorthodox orthodoxy, as, for example, in his treatment of the virgin birth. All three have been greatly misunderstood—the first two due mainly to the inability of English-speaking theologians to perceive the true nature of Barth's enterprise, and their consequent precipitous rejection of it; the third, due more to Barth's own statement.

A theology of the Word, according to the tradition of the Reformation, is always essentially a *corrective* theology. Like a teacher, it attempts to inform and transform by *confronting* the student, not by indoctrinating him. Only thus can the teaching of the Church become an event that stands witness to the grace of God, instead of a rigid instrument of propaganda. The task of the theologian is constantly to awaken the Church to this responsibility which alone is hers. And this does not always mean maintaining the tradition or a specific doctrine, however hallowed they may be. It means also criticism, that is to say, correction. For this reason some twenty years ago, reviewing in *The Christian Century* the development of his thinking, Barth could write: "My new task was to take all that has been said before and to think it through once more and freshly and to articulate it anew as a theology of the grace of God in Jesus Christ. I cannot pass over in silence the fact that in working at this task—I should like to call it a Christological concentration—I have been led to a critical (in a better sense of the word) discussion of church tradition, and as well of the Reformers, and especially of Calvin." • Of such an aim, this book offers the reader a concise and vivid realization.

However, it is from the standpoint of the Church that Barth conceives and conducts his theological task of correction, as is evidenced by the fact that he altered the title of his (nearly completed) *magnum opus* from *Christliche* (Christian) to *Kirchliche Dogmatik* (Church Dogmatics). But for him the Church is the *world-facing* reality which is brought about by the Word of God proclaimed and heard. She is not a world-denying sphere of hygienic righteousness. Only as a theologian of the Word, therefore, is Barth a theologian of the Church, that is, a man who took his "glorious liberty" seriously when he declared that he had been impelled to become *"simultaneously* very much more churchly *and* very much more *worldly."*

It is time to dispel the erroneous conception that Barth has no use for the things of this world and that like Tertullian he finds nothing in common between Athens and Jerusalem. Similarly, we must resist the widespread opinion, based on misinterpreted and extrapolated utterances from his earlier theological writings, that the lapidary formula "God is all, man is nothing" gives the real measure of his thinking. To be sure, these misreadings were further strengthened by Barth's categorical rejection of general revelation (i.e. his

---

• "How my mind has changed," *The Christian Century,* September 20, 1939.

rejection of the idea that God apart from Jesus Christ reveals himself also in nature and this, therefore, implies innate in man a "point of contact" or natural reciprocity between him and God). Strange as it may seem, in Barth's view, any attempt to establish a degree of similitude or resemblance between the Creator and the creature amounts to an implicit attitude of *contempt* for the creature. In preserving the radical *otherness* between God and man, Barth's intention indeed is to assert and preserve the inalienable condition of freedom and necessity which properly is man's. And in hinging his interpretation of this otherness on the Christ-event, he is led to the biblical conclusion that *in Christ* this otherness stands revealed as only one side of the coin, the other side being the fundamental *mutuality* between the Creator and the creature. Which means that God is not God without man; and were man nothing, God would not be all.

Thus there is, in Barth's theology, a point of contact between God and man. It is Jesus Christ. And there is also a point of contact between Athens and Jerusalem. Again, it is Jesus Christ. As Barth himself puts it, when the pagan, or, if you will, natural man hears about Jesus Christ it is of *his own* Lord that he hears.

All this goes to show that the "Christological concentration" which has governed Barth's theological method has led him, far from irrational fideism or anthropological pessimism, to the constant theme of God's own consistency with himself, i.e. with his intention and purpose as Creator, and to the theme that here and now the life-abundant is a possibility. "We must—even if it seems "dangerous"—affirm that the glory of God and the glory of man, although different, actually coincide. There is no other glory of God (this is a free decision of his will) than that which comes about in man's existence. And there is no other glory of man than that which he may and can have in glorifying God. Likewise God's beatitude coincides with man's happiness. Man's happiness is to make God's beatitude appear in his life, and God's beatitude consists in giving himself to man in the form of human happiness." The virtue of this "Christological concentration" is to show also that the ecclesiastical frame of reference of his *Dogmatics*, instead of calling for withdrawal from the world, actually constitutes a potent antidote to all forms of monasticism, asceticism, pietism, or perfectionism.

If any proof should be required in support of these assertions, it is to be found in the significance Barth attaches to the fact that, contrary to the traditional methods of dogmatics, he does not begin with general and epistemological considerations about the existence of a supreme being and a general knowledge of God. Right off, Barth begins with the reality of God which precedes and founds the reality of man, including man's *charismatic* (i.e. created by grace) capacity to know God and serve him.

Another evidence is furnished by the fact that Barth has treated ethics as part and parcel of his systematic theology, more exactly as the logical and Christological extreme point of his Church-centered dogmatic inquiry. Not only did this surprise everybody, but even more especially it caught unawares all those who had predicted that Barth-ianism and ethics would not mix. The inclusion of his ethical teaching within his theological teaching means for Barth nothing other than the exclusion of anthropological pessimism and cultural obscurantism, although it does not mean either one-sided optimism or unconditional surrender to automatic progress. This inclusion means that in the Christ-event God is God *for* man and that his faithfulness to his creation includes and grounds the possibility of human existence, not unlike the sun which shines on the just and on the unjust. Finally it means that a theologian's responsibility with regard to the ethical problem does not represent some concession—in the form of an afterthought—to the necessities and predicament of life in this world, as if faith required a chasm between certain sacred aspirations of man and his more realistic appraisal of secular and corrupt realities. This amounts to saying that Barth's view of man is not dichotomous. Nor is there for him a necessary antimony between that which is Christian and that which is not. The manner in which Barth exhibits this is itself very illuminating. In his *Dogmatics,* his first discussion of ethics occurs even before he has discussed anthropology. This points to two things. On the one hand, it implies that every kind of dichotomous view of the nature of man is based on the assumption of a golden age prior to the fall of Adam. Barth does not believe in any golden age. There was a sinner as soon as there was a man. On the other hand, this implies that the fundamental and only distinction is to be drawn between the Creator and the creature. Therefore, to say that there was a sinner as soon as there was a man means not to uphold a pessimistic view of man so much as to avoid all dichotomies such as Christian and non-Christian, the Church and the World, sacred and secular. In fact, Barth himself wrote in the forementioned article published in *The Christian Century:* "The abstract transcendent God, who does not take care of the real man ('God is all, man is nothing!'), the abstract eschatological awaiting, without significance for the present, and the just as abstract Church, occupied only with this transcendent God, and separated from state and society by an abyss—all that existed, *not* in *my* head, but only in the heads of my readers and especially in the heads of those who have written reviews and even books about me."

It was pointed out above that Barth's creativity partly consists in his ability to disclose bold, new meaning in ancient doctrines, and in his boldness —or, rather, theological and existential humility— in sticking to these doctrines. A striking example of this is his discussion of the virgin birth.

In connection with this doctrine, first of all Barth distinguishes (a) the mystery of the incarnation from (b) the miracle of the virgin birth, which is "the *sign* of that mystery." Once again, it is not surprising that he should start with the mystery of the incarnation and then only proceed to the miracle itself. This is in keeping with his theological method of speaking, for example, first of God's reality and revelation and then secondly of the possibility of his presence in his creation and of his availability to cognition.

What this mystery means is that "it guarantees

the efficacy of revelation." That is to say, it is God who takes the initiative and seeks man—not the other way round. It is *God* who becomes man: the basic distinction between Creator and creature nevertheless is here maintained, and no confusion is effected between them. But in the mystery of the incarnation it is their *unity* or mutuality which is equally stressed, because it is God who becomes *man*. The reality of the former statement is, so to speak, confirmed and sealed by the latter. As W. H. Auden says, "the Unknown seeks the known," and now God is no longer to be sought after.

But it is when we come to the second consideration, the miracle itself as *sign* of the mystery that Barth seems to lean too conspicuously towards orthodoxy (despite his warnings) and ultimately to deny his own premises, whereby the encounter between the Creator and the creature is initiated always by the Creator and is ever independent of the merit or demerit of the creature; whereby, through the Christ-event there is unity without confusion between them; and whereby the transcendence of the Creator upholds both the finiteness and transitory preeminence of the creature without ever implying contempt for him.

Barth puts this by saying that the action of the Holy Spirit means exclusion of human sin. Not that, he writes, "the sexual realm is the receptacle of sin. Such an interpretation, so characteristic of the Christian culture smacks of the cloister, the monks. Sexual asceticism is a pagan and not a biblical idea." That is to say, here again, the precedence of God is established both in his distinction from and his unity with man. "God excludes man, the fallen sovereign. For it was he,

Adam, who was called a sinner, although in the history of sin the woman played no little role, since she was the first who discussed theology! It is Adam, the glorious man and maker of history, who is deemed improper for God's designs. God steps into the act in Adam's place. *Not that he becomes husband to the woman, but through the action of his Holy Spirit he renders Joseph useless*" (italics ours). So far, to use Barth's categories, it is as if he were saying that the virgin birth is to the mystery of the incarnation what the sign is to that which is signified; and in this sense the exclusion of man as only the exclusion of sin, and a sign that all depends on grace, might be accepted.

But that the exclusion of sin necessitates the exclusion of the male specifically, is a distortion of the relation between sign and that which is signified, especially as Barth adds that God is not to be regarded as husband to the woman. Indeed, on Barth's own theory, only *charismatically* is there any concurrence between the sign and that which is signified: "the sign does not prove the thing signified, it communicates it. *In other words, this miracle was not necessary for the incarnation.* God could have chosen another process, even as Jesus could have done other miracles to signify the same Word. Hence the distinction between sign and the thing signified must be maintained" (italics ours). Our question is: Why, if Joseph is rendered useless, although God does not become husband to the woman, is not the miracle also rendered useless, since it is not necessary for the incarnation? The point is, in other words, that Barth does not sufficiently account for the charismatic character of the sign, namely that the sign is not to be confused with that which is signified, and that it may (on Barth's own view) point to that which is signified whether it has or has not any aptitude *of its own* for this. To be sure, there is "the danger that, by eliminating the sign, we thereby eliminate the thing signified." But Barth seems, on the other hand, to surrender the thing signified wholly to the sign, and to make the former dependent on the latter. One must wonder whether at this point there is not a tinge of *opus operatum* in Barth's understanding of God's grace. The tradition of the Reformation has always affirmed the relation between Creator and creature, or between the sign and that which is signified, in such a fashion as to reject explicitly every *opus operatum,* and the *analogia entis* (i.e. analogy of being between God and man) which this presupposes. It is therefore all the more strange that despite the existentially relevant illuminations of his *theological* interpretation, Barth should be compelled to uphold the *exegetically* defective traditional dogma of the virgin birth. From our vantage point, it appears that for Barth the miracle is to the Christ-event what the Garden of Eden is to the Fall, namely a golden age. Why does Barth reject one and seek refuge in another, especially since he implies that in their Eden Adam no less than Eve was discussing bad theology? The answer probably lies in his fear of natural theology.

Barth excised natural theology. He should now excise his fear of it and allow full expression of the motif of grace in which his theology has otherwise been so triumphant.

Finally, one of the pleasant tasks of a translator is to extend his gratefulness to those whose help has contributed to a richer and faithful rendering of the text. This was all the more difficult because Barth was expressing himself, not in his native German, but in French, which though grammatically correct is nevertheless idiomatically as Barthian as his *Dogmatik*. I am indebted to Mr. Robert Matthews for many suggestions at the stage of the first draft. I am more than indebted to my colleague Mr. Paul Ramsey, Harrington Spear Paine Professor of Religion at Princeton: always available, his assistance was all the more needed because of his knowledge of Calvin and Barth, and because of his friendship for myself. Thanks are also due to Mr. Arthur A. Cohen, publisher, for his careful reading of the manuscript and his many corrections. Grateful acknowledgment is, finally, extended to the Westminster Press for permission to quote the Catechism from Calvin's *Theological Treatises,* volume 22 of the *Library of Christian Classics.*

PRINCETON UNIVERSITY
April, 1958

PREFACE *by Jean-Louis Leuba*

At the invitation of the pastors of the Val-de-Travers (Neuchâtel), Mr. Karl Barth, professor at the Theological Faculty of the University of Basle, gave at Travers, on October 2 and December 30, 1940, then in Neuchâtel, on March 31, 1941, March 30 and October 5, 1942, January 11, 1943, six seminars on the first part of the Catechism of Calvin, that is, on the Reformer's explanation of the Apostles' Creed. We publish herewith, with Professor Barth's approval, an adaptation—the closest possible to the "spoken text"—of the stenographic notes taken during these seminars. The origin of this text will account for and, if necessary, excuse its peculiar style, now harsh, now spontaneous. In other respects, it is the very condition of the rich and numberless vistas into Calvin, the Creed and the biblical revelation which Mr. Barth has laid open for his listeners and will open, we hope, for his readers.

23

GENERAL INTRODUCTION TO THE CATECHISM •

Questions 1-7

QUESTION 1. What is the chief end of human life?—
That men should know God by whom they were
created.

In the language of his time, and in Calvin's own
language, "end" does not only mean what comes
last and might be static, motionless, but what keeps
man company throughout the course of his life.
End is thus equivalent to "sense•• of life," "goal
of life." It is not a terminus to life: it is a continuous action. And this action is "to know God"; it
is the primary end, but not the only one. There

• The catechism is quoted from Calvin's *Theological Treatises* Volume 22 of THE LIBRARY OF CHRISTIAN
CLASSICS; translated by the Rev. J. K. S. Reid and re-
printed with the kind permission of the Westminster
Press.

•• The French word "sens" signifies both "meeting"
and "direction." [Translator]

are secondary ends: family, country, profession, civilization, etc., but all these refer back to the primary end.

Before defining the knowledge of God, Calvin takes two indirect approaches so as to give us a better view of it.

QUESTION 2. What reason have you for saying so?—
Because he created us for this, and placed us in the world, that he might be glorified in us. And it is certainly proper that our life, of which he is the beginning, be directed to his glory.

Calvin considers the knowledge of God in relation to his glory. He states (objectively) that God is the beginning of our life and, from that, he infers (subjectively) that our life is senseless except in reference to his glory. In a word, we live for God's glorification. In the New Testament, to glorify signifies: to make either oneself or someone else appear such as he is; to show forth something in its essence; to reveal the secret either of one's own existence or of another's. The New Testament knows three kinds of glorification: a glorification of God by man (this Jesus Christ accomplishes), a glorification of man by God, and a glorification of God by God Himself. But the New Testament does not know of any glorification of man by man himself. Man may glorify only God and not himself, whereas God glorifies Himself and glorifies man. According to Genesis, God created man in His image, that is, in order that man may make God shine forth in his human existence.

Here, we must be specific. When we speak of glory, we always think of an exaggeration. Perhaps you are familiar with the inscription at Versailles:

"A toutes les gloires de la France" (To all the glories of France). Man's glory is like making a big noise, like trying to show off himself greater than he is. God does not need to make any fuss about his glory: God is glorious. He simply needs to show Himself as He is, He simply needs to reveal Himself. That is what He does in man, His creature, in whom He wants to be reflected. To live unto the glory of God then will be "necessary and reasonable": it will be the consequence of God's intention in creating man.

QUESTION 3.   What then is man's supreme good?— The very same.

Calvin makes here a distinction between what is reasonable and what is good. What is the chief good of man? What makes man happy? We know that reason (as we often define it) and happiness (as we fancy it) do not always go hand in hand. In his austerity Kant taught us the necessity of thinking only of the reasonable, and of despising happiness. Calvin, too, is an austere man, but for him reason and happiness agree. For him, the supreme reason and the supreme duty of man are identical with his supreme good, with his happiness. And this is man's happiness: to live for God's glorification.

QUESTION 4.   Why do you hold this to be the supreme good?—Because without it our condition is more unhappy than that of any of the brutes.

I understand this statement in this sense: if man did not accomplish his task of being God's mirror, he would be inferior to brute beasts. For brute beasts do (and the same can be said of the whole creation) accomplish God's intention in creating them. To be sure, they are not, like man, God's very image. But they have their destination, and they move towards it. If man misses his destination, he is inferior to the rest of creation. Not only beasts, but also stones, stars, insects, and all we see around us, leave us behind in this task of responding to the divine destination. Around us, praising is perpetual. The whole creation joins together in order to respond to God who created it. But man, in the midst of this chorus, of all this orchestra of creation, man stands still and does not do what he should do. This is man's misery: not to fulfill the meaning• of his creation.

> QUESTION 5. So then we clearly perceive that nothing worse can happen to man than not to live to God?—It is so.

This statement repeats and explains the meaning of Questions 3 and 4. Calvin resumes his exposition: Created to glorify God, we must know God so that we may and can glorify Him. One cannot live according to God without knowing God. To glorify God, to live according to God, hence is a conscious act, an act of the will; in a word, a human act. The humanity of this act resides in the very fact that it is based upon an act of knowledge.

After these two indirect approaches (Questions 2-5), Calvin now comes back to the knowledge of God (Questions 6-7).

•See note 1 p. 25. [Translator]

QUESTION 6. What then is true and right knowledge of God?—When He is so known, that His own proper honor is done Him.

The knowledge of God is not absolute, abstract knowledge, a knowledge important in itself. It is not knowledge for its own sake. This is such knowledge as has a direction, which is good for something, which has thus no value in itself, which does not have, or no longer has, a law of its own. "So to know God as to give Him honor": this knowledge has no value except that of its object, its task, its goal: to honor God. In itself it is nothing more than a service, and yet is all the more important because it does not have its importance in itself, but tends towards a goal that surpasses it: the honor of God which consists in glorifying Him.

So then, it would be absurd to speak of "Calvinistic intellectualism" with regard to the first Question. For the knowledge of God is not a self-satisfying science that might allow us to cut an important figure. It is a service that allows us to honor God.

QUESTION 7. What is the right way of honoring Him?—To put all our trust in Him; to study to serve Him all our life, by obeying His will; to call upon Him, whenever any need impels us, seeking in Him salvation and whatever good things can be desired; and lastly, to acknowledge Him with both heart and mouth to be the only author of all good things.

Once again: the knowledge of God is not a knowledge that leaves us untouched; it draws us along. God takes us into His service. He does not leave us as we were, and He does not let us "know" Him as though we were independent. He becomes All for us.

Calvin expounds in four points the right way of honoring God:

1. to put all our trust in Him; 2. to study to serve Him all our life, by obeying His will; 3. to call upon Him, whenever any need impels us, seeking in Him salvation and whatever good thing can be desired; 4. to acknowledge Him with both heart and mouth to be the only author of all good things.

These four points correspond to the four parts of the catechism and actually constitute its foundation:

1. *On the Articles of the Faith.* The content of the confession of faith calls for the response of man, his confidence in God, his faith, his "trust" (*fiance*) in God. Faith then is not only a state of the soul. It is an act founded upon the certainty of God's declaration.
2. *On the Law.* The law calls for the response of man, his service.
3. *On Prayer.* Here we learn how to "call upon" God in all our necessities.
4. *On the Sacraments.* Here, Calvin expounds how the sacraments are the God-ordained means for the sincere and visible witness of our faith and our service.

The catechism, as an exposition of the Revelation, gives us the object of knowledge. But this catechism ought to be accepted and considered as the true and right manner in which to accomplish our task and to actualize our human existence as God has intended it.

REMARK I. *On the Glory of God and the Glory of Man.* We must stress—even if it seems "dangerous"—that the glory of God and the glory of man, although different, actually coincide. There is no other glory of God (this is a free decision of His will) than that which comes about in man's existence. And there is no other glory of man than that which he may and can have in glorifying God. Likewise, God's beatitude coincides with man's happiness. Man's happiness is to make God's beatitude appear in his life, and God's beatitude consists in giving Himself to man in the form of human happiness. In this relationship between God's glory and man's glory, God's beatitude and man's happiness, we must note that God always has precedence: our glory is founded upon His glory; our happiness is founded upon His. God remains ever independent, master and sovereign. Man is only a servant. God gives, man receives. In other words, man cannot find in himself some divine thing and raise it into a god, or set up into divine beatitude some happiness he fancies by himself. Again in other words, man does not deserve what God gives him by pure grace.

God then is essentially love and grace. His mercy unto man is not merely an accidental thing: it is the essence of the divine heart.

God does not exist without this will to encounter us, to make us live and participate in Him. That is His steadfastness.

Now we come to the very crux of the matter: all we have said of God may only be said in the framework of the *Christian* knowledge of God. Apart from the relation between God and man such as it exists in Jesus Christ, all that we said would be equivocal and dangerous and even false. What was said about the relations between divine beatitude and human happiness, between the glory of God and the glory of man is then not an abstract truth: it is the explanation of the basic theses of Christology. What we say concerning the relationship of God and man, we say it in Jesus Christ. It is first in Christ that there is coincidence of divine glory and human glory. It is in him that the encounter between divine beatitude and human happiness takes place. There is no humanity "in relation to God" that was not first realized and prefigured in Jesus Christ. In Jesus Christ, true God and true man, this coincidence is realized, and with him rests our hope for a real humanity. Not by ourselves, but insofar as we are members of the Body of Christ— and thus only—we are men according to God. In order to avoid the misfortune of mankind's being lost because it does not fulfill the meaning of its creation, in order to be man, in order to fulfill the true humanism, then we must believe in Jesus Christ. There is no humanism without the Gospel.

REMARK II. *On the Precedence of God.* The four parts we have distinguished in Question 7 are answers to God's revelation. That is to say, there is no "a priori" human knowledge of God, there is no absolute theology. There is only, there can be only, a relative theology: relative to God's revelation.

God precedes and man follows. This act of following, this service, these are human thinking concerning the knowledge of God. Consequently in theology it will positively be necessary to refuse to accept any philosophical theory as a norm of theology. There is only one norm and it is: God who speaks. Not that we should not philosophize at all! We may—a little. There is choice irony on God's part which tells us: Since you have philosophy in you, well, then, have it and do your best with it. On the condition, however, that when you have to make a decision between your philosophy and some requirement of the faith, you always make sure that the subject precedes and human thought follows. On the condition that your philosophy does not keep you from "following." Calvin and Luther were Platonists enough. Later on, in the seventeenth century, everybody became Aristotelian. However, that did not keep these theologians from being faithful. But in the eighteenth century, they took to philosophizing without mincing words, and theology was no longer referred primarily to its subject, to God's revelation, but to such and such philosophy. They did not follow any longer; they wanted to begin all by themselves.

REMARK III. *The Four Calvinistic Absolutes.* It would be interesting to compare the other parts of Calvin's catechism with the four absolutes of the Oxford Group. Let us merely point out that all those of Calvin refer to God first, and only in the second place to man. God gives Himself to us as the object of trust and obedience, of request and praise. Then he demands these responses from us and enables us to present him with them, for our glory and happiness.

SPECIAL INTRODUCTION: THE "TRUST" • IN GOD

Questions 8-14

QUESTION 8. Now to consider these things in order and explain them more fully—what is the first head in this division of yours?—That we place all our trust in God.

"Fiance" (trust, confidence) comes from the Latin "fiducia." Fiducia is a term of jurisprudence: it designates the act whereby a person transfers a property to another without securing a written receipt from him; he thus presumes that the other person is trustworthy and will give back the property, although that person is not bound by any formal commitment. The "fiducia," for instance, is used in Roman law, for a nominal sale: the nominal seller must have confidence in the nominal buyer who could, if he is not of good faith, legally keep the fictitiously received property. To have all "confidence" in God, therefore, will mean: to entrust this blessing which is our life to the good will of God without any material promise on his part. We only have His word, only the confidence in His given word. We have given ourselves to him, so to say, in an unconditional surrender (*à corps perdu*) and it is up to him that we keep faith. We can do nothing to force him into giving back this gift

---

• *Fiance,* an old French term, meaning trust and confidence. [Translator]

entrusted to him. But we trust him to care for it. God alone can be the object of such a "fiance," such a total, absolute, complete trust. There are other "trusts," for example between this and that man, or between a man and his ideals; but no one except God deserves all our "trust" and no one is entitled to claim it from us. It would be erroneous on our part to put our whole "trust" in anyone other than God. For God alone deserves it, as He also demands it. "Trust" is then the essence of faith. Remember the first question of the Heidelberg catechism: "What is thy only comfort in life and death?—That I, with body and soul, both in life and death, am not my own, but being belong to my faithful Savior Jesus Christ." • The constant happiness and strength and security of the faith rest in this realization: I am in God's hands, and it is good that I am not in my own but in His hands. I have "trust" that God disposes better of myself than I could.

But Calvin does not stop at defining "trust" as the condition of all our knowledge of God. He now examines how we can win this "trust" (Questions 9-12).

QUESTION 9. How is this done?—When we know Him to be mighty and perfectly good.

It is unnatural to us, it is not inherent in us to have this trust. These two things are essential: that we should know God as both almighty and all-

---

• English text after "Aid to the Heidelberg Catechism" by James I. Good, D.D., Central Publishing House, 2060-2975 W. 25th Street, Cleveland, Ohio, 1904.

good. We must know whether He is so mighty that our property is in good hands and whether He is so good that this property is better off there than with us.

> QUESTIONS 10-11. Is this enough?—Far from it. Why?—Because we are unworthy that He should exercise His power to help us, or for our salvation show us how good He is.

Supposing even that there exists an almighty and all-good being, it is not yet certain that we might and could put in him all our trust. "We are unworthy." In other words: we cannot enjoy his almightiness and his all-goodness. It might be that this power and even this goodness could turn against us. The relationship between God and man, for Calvin, is then not simply one that unites a big being to a small one, an infinite being to a finite being. There is a personal rapport, there is a question of worthiness of the one unto the other. It is a moral and not only a physical relationship. The events that have come to pass between these two beings show that there was unworthiness on our part.

> QUESTION 12. What then is needed further?—Just that each of us should affirm with his mind that he is loved by Him, and that He is willing to be his Father and the Author of his salvation.

To this moral unworthiness of man corresponds the love of God. But no more than our unworthiness is God's love a description, a sort of natural history of our relations with him. It is a question of a history, of something which has come to pass in time, of a relationship of will and love: God loves, God wills—this is how Calvin expresses himself. There is will, there is love—this is how a philosopher would express himself. With the latter, truth is abstract; with the former it is an historical reality.

With Questions 13 and 14, Calvin examines how we can arrive at the certitude that God loves us.

QUESTIONS 13-14.   Where will this be apparent to us?—In His word, where He reveals His mercy to us in Christ and testifies of His love towards us.
Then the foundation and beginning of faith in God is to know Him in Christ? (John 17:3)—Quite so.

Calvin clearly indicates the origin of our knowledge of God's love. Note well: it is not a question of a general and abstract and philosophical knowledge, not a question of a treatise on the love of God in nature or on love in general; all this, all these abstract ideas are a piece of paper, a great noise, only ideas. The Gospel, on the contrary, tells us about realities. The task of theological reflection and of preaching does not begin at all with abstract ideas, but with the reality of God's action. The love of God is not an abstract quality of God's; it is an act: God takes to heart our misery. In Jesus Christ, He declares His mercy unto us and puts this mercy to work, and there is no mercy towards us outside Jesus Christ.

Here it is almost impossible for us not to run against our philosophical habits of mind. We indeed say, "Why could God's love not reveal itself otherwise?" May it not be that Jesus Christ is at most an intermediary who tells us about God's love, and afterwards becomes useless? In so thinking, we avow ourselves sons of the whole theological generation of the last two centuries, from J. F. Osterwald down to our time: according to that theology, Jesus Christ merely reveals to us an idea, the love of God, which we could have by ourselves. Between man and God there lies a fundamental relation: the adoration, the service of God. But who is God? What is that service? It is that which we are not told. It already smacks of Oxford Group ideas . . . God is supposed known. Jesus Christ comes only afterward, and at bottom we do not very well see why.

For Calvin, on the contrary, Jesus Christ holds a central position. There is not an "essence" of God's love that one could know as such, and then a "manifestation" of such a love whose eminent representative is Jesus Christ. No distinction is made between the principle and the person, between the message and the messenger. *Jesus Christ is what he brings forth.* He is the mercy of God, he is the love of God, he is the open heart of God. By knowing Jesus Christ, we then have this "trust" we talked about above. It is not only a possibility, it is a reality: "Therefore since we are justified by faith, we have peace with God" (Rom. 5:1). In the presence of Jesus Christ there no longer is any other alternative but to "trust" in Him.

REMARK I. *On the Precedence of "Trust."* The first point consists in reliance on the good will of God. You realize how fitting it is to be cautious when one asserts the stiffness and severity of Calvin. Precisely it is Calvin who begins with the Creed, and not with God's demands upon us, as revealed in the law. Calvin does not begin by saying to us: This is what you should be! He begins by saying: We are enabled to put our whole life in God's hands through Jesus Christ. And this life has been put there by this same Jesus Christ. We have this "trust" (which is far from saying merely: let us have this "trust").

REMARK II. *On the Authority of the Word.* To "trust" in God is not taking a chance, leaping into the darkness, or gambling and betting. For the Word of God is the very revelation of God, and the revelation of God is the demonstration of God. On the basis of that demonstration we have this "trust"—a "trust" that is not out of whimsey but an act of true wisdom.

REMARK III. *On the Conjunction of God's Almightiness and All-goodness.* Nothing is more frequent than to speak, on the one hand, of our knowledge of God's almightiness (nature, various events) and, on the other, of our knowledge of His goodness (Jesus Christ). There would thus be an almightiness of God which has nothing to do with his all-goodness, with the Christ. And there would be a goodness of God which is not almighty. It must rather be understood that almightiness and all-goodness are united in Christ. A good many errors of the religious life come from their separation.

INTRODUCTION TO THE APOSTLES' CREED

Questions 15-20

QUESTIONS 15-16. Now I would hear from you in a few words what the sum of this knowledge is. —It is contained in the confession of faith, or rather in the formula of confession, which all Christians hold in common. It is commonly called the Apostles' Creed, because from the beginning of the Church it was always received among all the pious, and because either it came from the lips of the apostles or was faithfully collected from their writings.
Repeat it.—I believe in God the Father Almighty, Maker of heaven and earth; and in Jesus Christ His only Son our Lord, who was conceived by the Holy Ghost, born of the Virgin Mary, suffered under Pontius Pilate, was crucified, dead and buried; He descended into hell; the third day he rose again from the dead, he ascended into heaven, and sitteth on the right hand of God the Father Almighty; from thence he shall come to judge the quick and the dead. I believe in the Holy Ghost; the Holy Catholic Church; the communion of saints; the forgiveness of sins; the resurrection of the body; and the life everlasting. Amen.

The substance of this knowledge is the Creed in its entirety. Therefore the whole Creed refers to our knowledge of God in Jesus Christ. Jesus Christ does not appear "in the second act" only. He is unceasingly present, unceasingly active.

QUESTIONS 17-18. To understand the several points more thoroughly—into how many parts shall

we divide this Confession?—Into four principal
parts.
Name them to me.—The first refers to God the
Father; the second concerns His Son Jesus
Christ, and also includes the entire sum of man's
redemption. The third part concerns the Holy
Spirit; the fourth the Church and the divine
benefits vouchsafed to it.

I do not wish to insist on the question of the
division of the Creed. Calvin—following the example of medieval scholasticism—counts four
articles. Sometimes, however, only three articles
were counted, integrating the Church and following affirmations under the third, that of the Holy
Spirit.

QUESTIONS 19-20. Since there is no God but one,
why do you here mention three, Father, Son
and Holy Spirit?—Because in the one essence
of God it is proper to regard God as beginning
and origin, the first cause of all things; then the
Son, who is his eternal wisdom; and last the
Holy Spirit, as his virtue diffused through all
things, which yet perpetually resides in himself.
You mean that there is no absurdity if in one
divinity we affirm these three persons, and that
God is not thereby divided?—Just so.

Nor will I insist on the doctrine of the Trinity.
Let us make only this remark: up to this point,
Calvin has made no attempt to say what God is.
No sooner is he forced to do so than he immediately speaks of the trinitarian God. Hence he does
not give any general doctrine of God. Later on,
in the seventeenth century, theologians begin with
a general theory of the divine essence (independ-

ence, wisdom, etc.). But for Calvin, none of the qualities of God can be named outside the frame-work of the trinitarian God. You perhaps remember that in the years 1536-38 Calvin was attacked as an antitrinitarian by M. Caroli, who besides was crazy. . . . Calvin was not antitrinitarian, yet we cannot be satisfied with his declarations on the Trinity in his Catechism and in the *Institutes*. We cannot, as Calvin does, portion out the quali-ties of God upon three persons: God the Father as the origin, the Son as wisdom, and the Holy Spirit as God's virtue. The persons in the Trinity are more than qualities in the Godhead. Calvin was suspected of adhering to the movement which con-fuses the three persons. Frankly, on this whole subject, I refer you to the first volume of my *Dog-matics*.

FIRST ARTICLE

Questions 21-29

The divisions of our text are clear enough and we shall follow them. There are six points: 1. What does God the Father mean (Question 22). 2. The question of God's Almightiness (Questions 23-24). 3. The creation of the world as God's work (Question 25). 4. Creation comprising heaven and earth (Question 26). 5. The notion of the Lordship of God over creation (Question 27). 5. The power of the opposition, of the devil, of evil, in the world, in its relation to the Lordship of God in this same world (Questions 28-29).

QUESTIONS 21-22. Repeat the first part.—I believe in God the Father Almighty, Maker of heaven and earth.

Why do you call him Father?—Primarily with regard to Christ, who is his eternal wisdom, be-

gotten of him before all time, and who, being
sent into the world, was declared his Son. From
this, however, we infer that, since God is the
Father of Jesus Christ, he is also our Father.

The term "to call" is not unequivocal. Is Calvin
thinking that perhaps God is not Father in himself, but simply is so called? This kind of thing,
it seems, is what Osterwald thinks: "Why do we
give God the title of Father?" (Mark the choice
of words: Father is here a title, a label pasted on
God.) Because he is the Maker and Master of all
things . . . Particularly we call him Father because he is the Father of our Lord Jesus Christ and
of the Christians.• Here it is quite clear: God is
not Father in himself, but somehow the term
Father qualifies him better than any other. This is
nominalism, that is, an attitude of man that allows
him to dispose of God. From human experience we
know what a father is and we apply this title to God.
On the contrary, the Bible, Calvin and the con-
fessions of the Reformation speak of God in the
manner of realism. If we call God Father, it is
because he is Father in reality. And the relation
between God's Fatherhood and fatherhood among
men reverses itself: we do not call God Father
because we know what that is; on the contrary,
because we know God's Fatherhood we afterwards
understand what human fatherhood truly is. The
divine truth precedes and grounds the human
truth. "For this reason I bow my knees before the
Father from whom every family in heaven and
earth is named" (Ephes. 3:14-15).

• J. F. Osterwald, *Catèchisme*, Genève, MDCII, p.
38 ff.

God is Father in respect to Jesus Christ. He is
Father in himself, and Jesus Christ is his eternal
Son. God expresses and represents himself ade-
quately. Between God and the Word he speaks
there is no difference; whereas there is a difference
between me and what I say. This Jesus Christ who
is the everlasting Word, who is the eternally begotten of God, has been manifested to the world.
He is God like his Father, and he is man like us,
with us, amidst us, man among men. Even as God
is Father with regard to Jesus Christ, so are we
men also in relation to Jesus Christ. In sum, God
is Father because he has a Son and we can be his
children because this Son stands for us before
him. We are not then being presumptuous when
we call God our Father, neither religiously auda-
cious, nor enthusiastic, nor sentimental. We are
simply being reverent. The Heidelberg Catechism
puts it even more clearly (Question 26): "What
believest thou when thou sayest, 'I believe in God
the Father Almighty, Maker of heaven and earth'?
—That the eternal Father of our Lord Jesus
Christ, who . . . made heaven and earth . . . is
for the sake of his Son, my God and my Father."
Not because he is almighty is God my Father. Because he is Father in himself. As Father he is almighty and as Father he is maker of all things. It
is very important to remember this in religious
education and in preaching so as not to awaken
the idea that God is only a father derivatively and,
so to speak, improperly.

QUESTIONS 23-24. In what sense do you accord him
the attribute almighty?—That not only he has
might he does not exercise; but that he has all

things under his power and hand; so that he governs the world by his providence, constitutes all things by his will, and rules all creatures as seems to him good. Then you do not suppose God's power to be inactive, but think it to be such that his hand is always engaged in working, so that nothing is done but through him and by his decree?—That is so.

Note first of all that the almightiness is mentioned only after the Fatherhood of God. That is to say, his almightiness is no abstract idea such as we often imagine when we say God "can do everything." We fall then into ridiculous riddles: can God lie? etc. These absurdities originate in a false beginning. God's almightiness should only be considered in the *exercise* of the almightiness, such as it is revealed to us in Jesus Christ.

In Jesus Christ, God is hidden and reveals himself. That is his almightiness. He is holy, and his holiness should not allow the creature to exist before him. He kills and makes us alive at the same time, he is merciful and he punishes. His very revelation of himself does not yield him into the hands of men: he remains free.

In Jesus Christ, God, out of the mercifulness of his heart, comes down from eternity, before the world is created. He bears all sins, all miseries and even death. He wills to suffer in his Son, and bearing in him all our sins, he wills to glorify himself. Victorious through the Cross, that is his almightiness.

In Jesus Christ, God, who is free, loves his creature; he who is above comes down below without ceasing to remain sovereign. Again, that is his almightiness.

In Jesus Christ, finally, God, who is the judge, the norm of man, judges us and at the same time pardons us. Again, that is his almightiness.

You see: the almightiness of God is not an abstract notion, not a power omnipotent in itself, a mad and profligate notion. But it is an action, an existence, a concrete manifestation of almightiness.

"All creatures are in his hand." Again this is not an idea, but an event. The expression "the hands of God" is no anthropomorphism. God disposes of men, governs and leads them. Even as he is the real Father, he also is he who has the real hands. We must beware of the idealistic spiritualism which makes us say: God is too much of a spirit to have hands. No, he has hands, the real hands (and not paws like ours . . .).

Finally, the almightiness of God is really almighty. We do not have to fear that there may be other kingdoms beside the kingdom of God: kingdom of the devil, kingdom of passions, evil, my bad behavior, my bad thoughts. Surely all these things exist, but not otherwise than subjected to God.

Thus is God continually at work: no off-seasons for God. He does not need to dream and sleep as we do, nor to take refuge in a world of fiction and fantasy. He is always he who allows and commands, and, in the words of the Heidelberg Catechism (26): ". . . I have no doubt (that) . . . he is able to do it, being almighty God, and willing, being our faithful Father." He will take care of us and will even change evil into good, not that evil as such becomes good, but by reason of God's work, evil is used unto good.

QUESTION 25. Why do you add: Maker of heaven
and earth?—Because he manifested himself to us
through his works, and in them he is to be sought
by us (Ps. 104; Rom. 1:20). For our mind is incapable of entertaining his essence. Therefore
there is the world itself as a kind of mirror, in
which we may observe him, in so far as it concerns us to know him.

We cannot know God in his essence. "No man
can see my face and live." But God makes himself
known to us in the world. Here we must make
several clarifications in order to avoid some big
mistakes.

First of all, the world, creation, is not a part
of God as the gnostics used to represent it. The
world is not an emanation from God, but the
putting into being of something different from
God, which is over against God. If the world
were divine in itself, it could not be said: God
loves the world, for then God would be loving
himself and remain alone. Love signifies: relationship between two really different beings. The
world is then a reality in itself, a proof of the
mercy of God who agrees to the existence of something outside of himself. There is an absolute
imparity between God and the world, but, within
this imparity, there is a hyphen: creation depends
on God. God upholds creation and God judges
what is good and what is evil. There is no good
and evil "in itself," but God judges good and evil.
And the sin of man consists precisely in the fact
that he himself wants to judge what is good and
what is evil.

Next, what is the nature of the knowledge of
God which is given us in the world? Let us beware

now: Man has no possibility to know God "through nature."

There is no knowledge of God which was given along with the existence and the essence of the world. We ourselves cannot say: God is in the world here or he is there. But God himself is he who, in the world, gives himself to our knowledge, according as he pleases. We notice with what reservations Calvin speaks of this knowledge: the world does not stand witness of God but insofar as God wills it and wherever he wills it. It is not the history of any people which witnesses unto God, but the history of Israel. It is not any book, but the Holy Scripture. It is not any man, but Jesus Christ. And yet the history of Israel, the Bible and Jesus Christ belong to the world. The world then is a mirror that reflects something found elsewhere, that reflects it insofar as God wills it and wherever God wills it.

QUESTION 26. By heaven and earth you understand, do you not, whatever creatures exist?—Yes, certainly; but in these two names are comprised all things, since they are either heavenly or earthly.

The Nicene Creed expresses it this way: "the visible and the invisible." We might add: ideas and matter, spirit and body, angels and beasts. Thus there is distinction between spirit and matter. But if there be a relative superiority of the spirit over matter, there is no absolute difference between them in relation to God: both spirit and matter are creatures and redemption applies as well to either. Let us not fancy that spirit is divine in itself, or that matter, unlike spirit, is not called to redemption. Let us not fancy that this is only an ecclesiastical problem: it is also a political problem. For all that is within the world is called to redemption. Spirit and matter are united both in sin and grace: let us not separate what God has united.

QUESTION 27. Why then do you call God merely creator, when it is much more excellent to defend and preserve creatures in their being, than once to have made them?—This term does not merely imply that God so created his works once that afterwards he took no care of them. Rather, it is to be held that the world, as it was once made by him, so now is preserved by him, and that similarly both the earth and all other things persist only in so far as they are sustained by his virtue and as it were his hand. Besides, since he has all things under his hand, it also follows from this that he is the supreme ruler and lord of all. Hence from his being Creator of heaven and earth, we are to understand that it is he only who with wisdom, goodness and power rules the whole course and order of nature; who is the author of both rain and drought, hail and other storms, as also of serenity; who fertilizes the earth of his beneficence, or again renders it sterile by withdrawing his hand; from him also both health and disease proceed; to whose power finally all things are subject and at whose nod they obey.

We have here the opposite of the parable of deism which says God made the world like the clockmaker a clock. Once all was finished, the clock works by itself, with no help from the clockmaker. On the contrary, God is maintaining his creation unceasingly. Nothing in the world is independent of God; where there is order, it is God-given. If there be chance or fate, these are still under God's governance. No necessity, no absolute action is independent of God, no freedom which is not God-granted (for he does grant it), no contingency which is not disposed of by God. The order existing in the world has nothing absolute about it. It does not exist aside from him who ordains. At bottom, both determinism and indeterminism are false: God governs and allows determinate and indeterminate things.

From our point of view as creatures, there are "good" things and "evil" things. But the certainty of the fatherly governance of God teaches us how to be thankful for whatever he sends our way. For all things are under his governance. The Heidelberg Catechism puts it even more positively (27): "All things come not by chance, but by his fatherly hand." Therefore there can be no need for a theodicy, no need to justify God in all he does, since everything that happens is in his hand and since good and evil cannot be judged "in themselves," but in relation to his fatherly goodness.

QUESTIONS 28-29. Now what shall we say of wicked men and devils? Shall we say that they too are subject to him?—Although he does not govern them by his Spirit, yet he checks them by his power, as with a bridle, so that they are unable even to move unless he permits them to do so. Further, he even makes them ministers of his will, so that they are forced, unwilling and against their inclination, to effect what seems good to him.

What benefit accrues to you from the knowledge

of this?—Very much. For it would go ill with us, if anything were permitted wicked men and devils without the will of God; then our minds could never be tranquil, for thinking ourselves exposed to their pleasure. Only then do we safely rest when we know them to be curbed by the will of God and, as it were, held in confinement, so that they cannot do anything but by his permission, especially since God himself undertakes to be our guardian and the captain of our salvation.

Calvin does not explain the origin of evil. It suffices him to state it. God and his creation are the grand "Yes" whereto any opposite is "no." But as for this evil, God puts a bridle upon it. Consequently we must not run through the world with sad faces, with "momiers'" looks.• We believe too much in the strength of the devil, we bury Christ again after his resurrection.

All we have said is not a "Weltanschauung," a theory, some thing to be contemplated. It is faith: that is, not an idea about God, but a relationship with God who is acting and whose action in Jesus Christ grounds our trust.

• "Momier" (same root as mummy?) was a nickname given in the early 19th century to bigoted revivalists of French-speaking Switzerland. [Translator]

SECOND ARTICLE

Questions 30-37

I. INTRODUCTION TO THE SECOND ARTICLE

The second article treats of Jesus Christ. Before we tackle it we shall make two general remarks:

REMARK I. *On the Link Between the Three Articles of the Creed.* The first article speaks of God, the father of Jesus Christ. God is God, above man. Already then, we had to speak of man. And in the third article, that of the Holy Spirit, we shall see that it deals again with God, but along with man, within man. The second article tells us: God himself is man. Therefore it is central, and from it we must interpret both the first and the third. The second article forms the pivot of this God-man relationship expressed also in the first and the third. In sum, it expresses the content of the whole

Creed. The first article is only the presupposition of the second, and the third is its consequence. Thus, in the Christian sense, we may speak of God "in himself" only after we have understood his divine condescension whereby he became man in Jesus Christ. And, likewise, we cannot speak of the Christian "in himself," for the Christian is only a consequence of that unity of God and man in Jesus Christ. Every theological error could be reduced to two basic types: an abstract theology of man, or, more exactly, of the man Jesus Christ (rationalism) and an abstract pneumatology of God in Jesus Christ, a "spiritualistic" doctrine which treats of an anonymous "Spirit" (various mysticisms, of which perhaps the most characteristic is Buddhism).

If so, if the second article is central and capital and, in a word, primary, we might wonder why the Creeds of the early Church have the order: Father, Son and Holy Spirit; creation, redemption, sanctification. Two interpretations ought to be rejected at once: The point is not the order of experiences. One does not begin by understanding creation, then redemption, then sanctification. For one understands creation solely in Jesus Christ. Creation understood first by itself would never lead to redemption or to sanctification. No, if one wants to speak on the basis of experience, one should begin with the third article, that of the Holy Spirit who enlightens our hearts so that we understand both redemption and creation. Neither is the point the order of factual importance. For then we should begin with the second article. No, the point is rather the order of God's essence, that is, of God's Trinity. To these statements, we may well add that the order has nothing immutable about it. (Cf. II Cor. 13:13 where the order is: Jesus Christ, God the Father and Holy Spirit.) The important thing is that false consequences are not drawn from this order.

REMARK II. *On the Calvinistic Interpretation of the Second Article.* In this connection we shall distinguish three points:

a) Calvin continually and closely notes *the relation between the second and the third article.* He was not as clear on the relation between the first and the second. Surely, the first article presupposes and already calls forth the second. But the second does not explicitly recall the first. On the contrary, not only does the second call forth the third, but the third recalls the second. The doctrine of Christ and that of the Holy Spirit are linked together. (This is found again in the *Institutes* III. 1.) This union between pneumatology (doctrine of the Holy Spirit) and Christology (doctrine of the Christ) means that Christ is not separated from the work of Christ. There is intimate connection between what Christ is and what he does. This is the reason why Calvin, even before he treats of the two natures, treats of the office of Christ. In other words, to know Christ, for Calvin, necessarily implies the knowledge of Christ's past, present and future work. But one does not remain in a framework that is, so to speak, merely historical. What came to pass there and then, comes to pass here and now, *hic et nunc.* In other words again, Christ is not isolated, but he immediately is with his own, his members, with the Church.

Nor can one speak of Christ's own without calling in at once all the substance of Christ himself. It was our death and our life that were unfolded on Golgotha and at the Resurrection, two thousand years ago. In this respect Calvin, far from innovating, only conveys what the early Church taught.

b) If we study what Calvin tells us of Christ, we shall notice that *he does not give us any abstract definition of his manhood and his Godhead, nor of their relations. But he shows us the succession of the FACTS:* the fact that Jesus Christ is not only a man, or the fact that his Godhead is hidden under his manhood, or the fact that he glorifies his manhood by his Godhead. And showing them to us, Calvin invites us to follow these facts. He bids us enter into the history of Christ. The same holds for Christ as it does for a bird in full flight. No picture will convey that flight, except a moving picture. Likewise in theology: you will understand nothing if you try to lay hold of a position, to apply your mind to an assertion. You must follow the positions, follow the assertions and view the whole, not as if it were a system, but as a history. And the Christians are members of the cast of that history. And their small stories exist only as referring to that great history. For this reason, Calvin does not expound an explicit doctrine of the two natures of Christ. Instead he treats them as he proceeds along the *movement* of the question: How can he be called Son of God since we are all children of God? Likewise, he does not treat abstractly his manhood, but (Questions 50-51) in relation to the *story* of Mary. In sum, we meet again what we expressed in the first point. Calvin does not tell us what Christ is without telling us what he does. He does not tell us of his being without telling us of his life. He does not tell us of his person without telling us of his office.

c) When we grasp each position simply within the movement of the whole, it can also be rightly remarked that *we grasp the whole in each position* (even as each note of a melody contains the entire melody). For example, it is almost impossible to mark any difference for Calvin between the significance of Christ's death from that of his resurrection. Death already contains the hidden victory, and the resurrection is a victory just because it throws death into relief. The movement from death to resurrection does not increase but reveals the substance of the matter.

II. THEOLOGY OF THE NAME AND TITLE OF JESUS CHRIST

Questions 30-45

QUESTIONS 30-31. Now let us come to the second part.—It is that we believe in Jesus Christ his only Son our Lord.
What is principally contained there?—That the Son of God is our Savior; and at the same time is expounded the means by which he has redeemed us from death, and procured life.

As was pointed out, in our introduction, these few words contain the whole Creed.

In the following, it may seem curious to us that Calvin had the idea of explaining the name "Jesus" and the title "Christ." These things are important for him. For the early Church, it was not arbitrary or meaningless to pronounce the two words: Jesus Christ. This meant more than mentioning a name. This name says everything that was to be said. You perhaps know that one of the oldest creeds contained only these three words: Jesus Christ Lord. The people who said this also thought it. Such an identification of the thing with the word comes no longer natural with us. We need to learn again from the Bible that the name is not only a name, but is the reality itself. In the Old Testament it is God's name (Yahweh) which differentiates him from other gods, the heathen gods. His name is God's means of "introducing himself," it is his revelation. That is why Moses demands that the name of God be revealed to him. The same holds for Jesus Christ, "the name which is above every name . . ." The same holds for the title. With us, a title such as minister or professor is an advertisement, a label. It is hardly more than pasted on the individual. But in the Bible, the title worn by people (in the Old Testament: prophet, king, priest; in the New Testament: evangelist, apostle) is the very essence of the holder's life. There are prophetical and apostolic and royal and priestly offices; and the various duties of his office fall, so to speak, upon a person and take possession of him. It is not the office which belongs to a person so that he may dispose of it at his discretion. But it is the person who belongs to the office: he was called to assume it. From the beginning of his existence, and even before, he was chosen to wear that title and to achieve what the title implies. Even though the person dies, the office will last on.

THE NAME OF JESUS

QUESTIONS 32-33. What does the name Jesus which
you apply to him mean?—It means what the
Greeks meant by the word σωτήϛ. In Latin there
is no proper name which rightly expresses its
force. Hence the term Savior was commonly accepted. Moreover, the angel gave this name to
the Son of God by the command of God himself
(Matt. 1:21). Does this mean more than if men
had given it to him?—Certainly. For since God
wished him to be thus named, it is necessary that
he be so forthwith.

The parents of Jesus, accordingly, did not have
the freedom to choose a nice name, a name which
would be interesting for men, bringing back mem-
ories of their life, etc. The name was given him
by God. And it is not simply a label. It is the
Savior's reality. In the name of Jesus, there is no
difference between "person" and "name." Rather,
this person *is* he who is named Savior. In this respect we suggest the two following considerations:
   a) When a Savior is spoken of, the necessity of
salvation is thereby implied. But Calvin did not
and would not say: he is savior because we know
we need to be saved, because of sin, death, and all
sorts of mean things. Calvin does not show us our
state of misery—that we can realize anyway—and,
then, Jesus who comes to meet us and whom we
call Savior because we happen to find him such. It
is not so! There is first of all, even before we understand that we need to be saved, there is the Savior. It is the Savior who reveals, who makes clear

to us the need to be saved. Hence we do not have to ask ourselves at first: What is man? Who are we? What do we think of Christ?

Rather we can follow the witness by which God brought the savior into existence. By reason of his name we have to accept what he is and consequently what we are. It is not a question of thinking first of ourselves and then of Christ, but of Christ then of ourselves.

b) If such is the case, the whole mystery, the whole miracle of the incarnation is announced through this name. We are saved at the very moment we learn we have a savior and thus that we are to be saved! Ours is a savior who reveals to us at once both our salvation and the perdition from which we are saved! A fact is then in question, and not an idea or a "religion" in which all mankind copes with its anxieties and its illusions time and again. Something came to pass, something comes to pass with this man who bears the name of Savior. Already now, we understand that faith in the name of Jesus is not a general knowledge of the relationship between God and man, but a direct relation between the believer and that person who bears the name of Savior. Faith is man's acceptance of the event which is brought about in that unique person of the Savior.

THE TITLE OF CHRIST

QUESTIONS 34-36. What force then has the name Christ?—By this epithet his office is even better expressed. For it signifies that he is anointed by his Father to be King, Priest and Prophet.

How do you know this?—Because Scripture applies anointing to these three uses; and also because it often attributes these three offices to Christ.

But with what kind of oil was he anointed?—Not with visible oil, such as was employed in the ancient anointings of kings, priests and prophets; but more excellently, that is by the grace of the Holy Spirit, which is the essence of that external anointing (Ps. 45).

He is the Christ, that is, the Anointed: according to the Old Testament, Calvin says, this means one who has received a certain office in the framework of God's Covenant with his people. (This office will be examined later on.) Now the important thing is the unction itself. Calvin studies it on the basis of the Old Testament. The Old Testament therefore contains a truth, but this truth points beyond itself: this truth announces the New Testament which, for this very reason, is already contained yet concealed in the same truth. Christ's unction then is the truth of all unction, and Christ's office is the truth of all office. Reciprocally, all the other unctions help us to understand what Christ's unction is.

But what is the substance of this unction? What is that truth of Christ which is the truth of the Old Testament? Calvin answers us. Here for the first time we meet with the relation: Christ and Holy Spirit, very important for the whole of Calvin's doctrine. When the Scripture speaks of the Spirit, it speaks of God himself, but in a certain way: God considered and understood in his freedom over against his creature, in his freedom to accept this creature of his, and to make a covenant with him, to open unto himself the hearts and the eyes and the ears of man, and to make man his child. That the creature should be living again before God is the issue: such is the work of the Holy Spirit. When we learn that Christ was anointed by the Holy Spirit, this means that it is Christ who is bearer of the Holy Spirit; it is he who has in himself this "mode of being" of God who turns, in his freedom, toward man to quicken him. (Cf. Michelangelo's painting where God's finger quickens man. The early Church used to call the Holy Spirit God's Finger.)

Any other unction, whatever there is of Holy Spirit in mankind outside Christ, can only be either a foreshadow or a consequence of the unique unction whose sole bearer is Christ. Thus we may very well say that the prophets, Moses and Abraham, had the Holy Spirit. Yet the real truth of their unction lies in Christ's unction. And they themselves disclose to our eyes, as in a splendid image, every aspect of Christ's unction.

The unction we are concerned with here is nothing other than the incarnation about which we will talk later on. The incarnation is the mystery of the Holy Spirit, and the Spirit is nothing other than the relation between God and his creation. In the Holy Spirit God is merciful and communes with mankind. God has no need to find himself in this communion, but out of his freedom he enters into contact with the world. This freedom is the freedom of his grace; hence it is a freedom in which, for our part, we have the freedom to put our trust.

In the election of this one man, we are invited to acknowledge our own election. And it must even be said that the whole world is here invited to acknowledge God's love. These two things must be carefully considered: the uniqueness of Christ and his significance for the whole world, the concentration and the universality of grace. It is *here* that grace is found, in Jesus Christ: but it is grace intended for the whole world, since it is grace.

RELATION BETWEEN THE CHRIST AND HIS OWN

QUESTIONS 40-41, 45. But do you reap any benefit from this?—Indeed all these things have no other purpose than our good. For Christ is vouchsafed these things by the Father, in order that he may share them with us, and out of this fulness of his we all draw (John 1:16).

Explain this to me a little more fully.—Christ was filled with the Holy Spirit and loaded with a perfect abundance of gifts, that he may impart them to us, according to the measure, of course, which the Father knows to be appropriate (Eph. 4:7). So from him as the only source we draw whatever spiritual blessings we possess.

All you have said, then, comes to this, that Christ's name comprises three offices which the Father conferred on the Son, that he might transfuse their strength and fruit into those who are his.—That is so.

We take up these questions now, because they show us Calvin's intention as he speaks of the office of Christ. Straight off and foremost, a real office is the issue, that is, a work Jesus does not do for himself. But in doing and in accepting all the graciousness of this work, he does so for our sake; he fulfills his work in order to make us participate in it, in order to be a fountain, in order to communicate the fruit and profit of his work to the faithful. In the title conferred upon him, even as in his name, the unity lies between Christ and his own, between the "head" and the "members." Through the Holy Spirit God gives and receives grace in Jesus Christ; then in turn we receive it. He gives, he receives, we receive; and that is the end. We do not have to "give back." For in him all is accomplished. And the Spirit who is between the Father and the Son also unites us to God: he is the principle of our unity with God.

In the Heidelberg Catechism (32), there is a certain broadening of what Calvin says in this connection: "But why art thou called a Christian? —Because I am a member of Christ by faith, thus am partaker of His anointing, that so I may confess His name, and present myself a living sacrifice of thankfulness to Him: and also that with a free and good conscience I may fight against sin and Satan in this life; and afterwards reign with Him eternally over all creatures." Between this and what Calvin says there is a difference not of principle but of nuance. Calvin limited himself to saying: we receive the Holy Spirit from Christ as from a fountain. *Heidelberg* adds that this "receiving" entails some consequences, that this acceptance is something active. That is, since the Christian has also received an unction through his participating in the anointing of Christ, this unction will not only consist in receiving but also in doing. On his level, if we dare say so, the Christian is a little Jesus Christ: by confessing the name of Christ, he repeats the office of prophet. By offering himself in sacrifice, he repeats the office of priest. By fighting against sin with a free conscience, he repeats the office of king. The Heidelberg Catechism had a right reason for insisting on this action of the Christian. For grace means not to lie on a chaise longue but to receive a motion. Of course, a specific difference persists between Christ and his own. Yet the office of Christ is being repeated through his own. To receive Christ is by the same token to be placed in the situation of a follower of Christ. A follower and not an imitator. To follow is to do *after* him. To imitate would be to do *as* he did. The Christian can then do only what Christ did before him: he will not do it with the same significance. His life will remain very human. But he will live "in the steps" of Christ as is said in the Epistle of Peter (I Peter 2:21).

We shall now examine the office of Christ and the office of the Christians, taking together what Calvin says of each.

THE TITLE OF KING

> QUESTIONS 37 and 42. But what kind of kingdom is it you mention?—A spiritual kingdom, contained in the Word and Spirit of God, which carry with them righteousness and life.
> What does his Kingdom confer upon us?—Just this, that by its benefit we are accorded freedom of conscience for pious and holy living, are provided with his spiritual riches, and also armed with strength sufficient to overcome the perpetual enemies of our souls, sin, the flesh, the devil and the world.

Jesus is king. He preserves and defends a dominion and its participants. To do so, he is just and living. Christ is mighty: this is the first thing Calvin says of Christ. Yet mighty through the Word and the Spirit of God. Power and might (real power and real might) are not for Calvin on a level with other than Word and Spirit. It is still too conventional in our surroundings to set up the contrast here that, on the one hand, might is evil, power is secular; while, on the other, Word and Spirit are fine things, but not nearly so powerful . . . No! Christ reigns—through the Word and through the Spirit. Everything that, we think, has some "power" (political or otherwise) is at bottom no power at all. What has real power, real might, real dynamism? The Word, the Spirit; these are almighty. Any other kind of power is but subjected to this power. The power of electricity, of the sea, or of the wind are like a parable of the power of the Spirit. At this point we are not yet concerned to explain the nature of the kingdom of Christ, what he does as a king. Rather, the important thing is first of all to understand that he reigns. He reigns alone and needs no one else to help him.

Then, Calvin applies this dominion to the Christians. A very interesting expression is found here: ". . . we are accorded freedom of conscience." The great phrase of the Revolution derives from this except that here it has another meaning altogether. "Freedom of conscience" comes from the fact that Jesus is present. That is all. It comes from the fact that he alone has all power, because in his Word and in his Spirit we have the sum of all possible power. Thus it is that his own are accorded freedom of conscience. They have nothing to fear. Nothing can ultimately threaten their security. The very term "conscience" leads us to the same understanding of things. Conscience, in Latin as in Greek, clearly means: to know with. With whom? With God. Man knows with God, he is found to agree with God. He knows what God knows, he knows the design of the sovereign and merciful God. If he meets with other powers, he does not fear them because he knows in his conscience, because he is conscious that those powers are subordinated to God (Cf. Rom. 8:38-39).

This is freedom of conscience. Such freedom is dependent on the Kingdom. "Where is the kingdom, says Christ, there is true conscience." I think it would be interesting to study more closely what are the historical and spiritual relations between Calvin and that good French Revolution. Who knows? Perhaps it is time for Christians to defend the French Revolution! In any case, under the Vichy government it is necessary to side with the freedom of consciences.

THE TITLE OF PRIEST

QUESTIONS 38 and 43. And the priesthood?—It is the office and prerogative of presenting oneself before the face of God to obtain grace, and of offering sacrifice, which may be acceptable to him, to appease his wrath.

What is the purpose of his priestly office?—First, that on this ground he is our mediator, who reconciles us to the Father. Then too, because through him there is opened up for us a way to the Father, so that with boldness we may come into his presence, and ourselves also offer in sacrifice to him ourselves and all we have. And in this way he makes us his colleagues in the priesthood (Heb. 7; 8; 9; 10; 13).

He is a priest who has the authority to stand before God. Man has this authority no longer. No longer is he in Paradise. In Paradise, he could talk with God, instead of hiding from him. Now it is different. And the priest, in the midst of men, is the man in whom appears, as if personified, man such as he ought to have been: he who stands upright before God, who obtains God's grace, who gives God what God wills. The Old Testament priests are not priests "in themselves." No man is priest "in himself." Rather Jesus Christ is the reality of all priesthood. It is in Christ that the Old Testament priests stood before God. It is in Christ that man stands before God, in Christ, man obeys God, in Christ, man can give something to God. Just as we can fight against and suffer anything because Christ is king, so we are able *to be* before God, to be reconciled with him, and to offer ourselves in sacrifice, because Christ is priest. We have become "acceptable," which we were not in ourselves. And, in Christ, we are in the state of offering something that God can accept from our hand.

THE TITLE OF PROPHET

QUESTIONS 39 and 44. Now in what sense do you call Christ prophet?—Because, when he descended into the world, he proclaimed himself an ambassador to men and an interpreter; and to this end, that by fully declaring the Father's will he might put an end to all revelations and prophecies (Isa. 61:1; Heb. 1:2).

There remains prophecy.—It is an office of teaching bestowed upon the Son of God for the benefit of his own; and its end is that he illumine them with the true knowledge of the Father, instruct them in truth, and make them household disciples of God.

The prophet is the man who is the messenger and sovereign ambassador of God, his father, commissioned to expound plainly God's will to the world. Jesus is this messenger and this ambassador. He declares the will of God. No man declares the will of God, except in terms of Christ, who is the only real prophet. The point is, therefore, that we must not fancy ourselves as "private" prophets; no, we do not need any new discoveries in the realm of the divine. All we need has been said and we have just to repeat it. To take part in the prophecy means for us to be pupils in the House of God. Such a wealth of riches is there that we should not regret that we are not, that we cannot be, prophets . . .

REMARK I. *On the Identity of the Person and the Work of Christ.* According to the Apostles' Creed, whatever Christ is he does. What comes next is simply the execution, the working out of what his name and title indicate. Therefore whatever is said about the birth, life, death, resurrection of Jesus Christ will simply repeat and explain this: he is king, priest, prophet of the Holy Spirit.

REMARK II. *On the Pre-eminence of Baptism over Birth.* According to Calvin's explanation, man—for Questions 40-44 deal with man himself—exists primarily in his status as Christian, then next (and only next) in his status as man and sinner. This is very interesting. Man comes on the stage as a Christian first, in the catechism, and not as a rational being, then as a sinful creature, next converted, next Christian, etc. In other words, *baptism is more important than our birth.* Man, for Calvin and the New Testament alike, exists by virtue of his baptism and not by virtue of his birth. Anything interesting to be said of man is what can be said of him in fellowship with Christ: he is, in some degree, a little king, a little priest, a little prophet. After that you'll see the beast in him and his defects! But first, he is the image of the Son of God. The fall comes only next. Gospel first. Then the Law.

REMARK III. *On the Relation of the Three Offices.* These three offices are not three departments, any more than are the three persons of the Trinity. While maintaining the difference between the three offices, their connection must be seen, since the one always implies the others. Christ is king. How? By being a prophet, says Calvin, that is, by being bearer of the Word and Spirit of life. He is a priest because he has power over everyone, and he needs this power to be a mediator. He is a prophet because he is king and speaks with authority.

III. ONLY SON OF GOD

Questions 46-47

QUESTIONS 46-47. Why do you apply the term only to the Son of God, when God deems us also worthy of the title?—That we are sons of God is something we have not by nature but only by adoption and grace, because God gives us this status. But the Lord Jesus, who is begotten of one substance with the Father, is of one essence with the Father, and with the best of rights is called the only Son of God (Eph. 1:5; John 1:14; Heb. 1:2), since he alone is by nature his Son.

You mean, then, that this honor is properly his as due to him by right of nature, whereas it is communicated to us by gratuitous favor, in that we are his members?—Precisely. Hence with regard to this communication, he is elsewhere called the first-born among many brethren (Rom. 8:29; Col. 1:15).

This assertion "Jesus Christ is the only Son of God" only stresses, but very strongly stresses, the content of his name and title. The assertion "only Son of God" helps to explain the mystery and reality of Christianity, *of that fellowship of men who by grace partake in the nature of God* (and all this must be stressed). Christians do not only partake in "something" divine or in something that, in the framework of mankind, may possess a certain superior quality. But they partake in the very nature of God. (Cf. 2 Peter 1:4.) By grace do they partake in it; not by nature. For we are not

God's children by nature. It is very important to make this point very clear. We are dealing with a reality: the reality of God in Jesus Christ. And this reality is conferred upon us. Were it not for this reality, why then, one would be left with some Christian "religion," that is, an enormous illusion —very pious, perhaps, very sincere to be sure, but no less an illusion.

This question is not theoretical; it is highly practical. It is God himself who acts through this king, this priest, this prophet. And what he has done as such is not an attempt at or an effort toward an ideal; it is reality itself. Jesus Christ is not only God's interpreter, he is the very text to be interpreted. While acting as chargé d'affaires, as ambassador, he was the person, the king, the sovereign he represented.

In order to understand the term "only *son*," it should next be remembered that in the Bible the term "son" means a being who belongs to someone or to something wherein he has his whole origin. A "son" is not to be understood otherwise than through what his father is and represents. In this sense, the child is equal to the father. If he is called *"only* son," it is for the purpose of insisting on the unique work of God. There are many works of God. But this one is the work of all works. There is no principle of creation, no human existence, no reality, outside Christ.

REMARK I. *On the Godhead of Jesus Christ.* By becoming man Jesus Christ remains what he is. He loses nothing of his Godhead. Incarnation by no means signifies a diminution of his Godhead. God does not cease to be God when he becomes merciful, when he shows forth his mercy. Such an immutable God, who "is what he is," is a Platonic idea, a nightmare of our former dogmatics. Yes, he is what he is, but he is the living and merciful one! Hence the humiliation of God must not be put in contradiction to his majesty. To surrender the absolute and essential Godhead of Jesus Christ amounts to surrendering God himself. Such is the meaning of the early Church's struggles. Modern theologians who mock the people of Constantinople disputing on whether Jesus Christ is analogous to God or God himself show themselves more stupid than they. For here is the knot of the question. The object of all the fourth century's discussions is very simple: the point was to express the fact that Christ alone originates in God and is unceasingly engendered of him (whereas the world is created and can separate from him). If God reveals himself, he reveals nothing other than himself. "God alone speaks well of God." His Son is the content of his revelation. No substitution takes place in his revelation, neither in its content nor in its form. God is the content, God is the form, God is the means.

Hence the Christ is, as Calvin says, the mediator, the qualified intermediary, because he was not someone from us who went to seek after God for us. Rather he was appointed of God himself. God has appointed himself as our advocate, our intercessor; it is God himself who speaks to God himself in our favor! This means that in the act of revelation, of redemption, of reconciliation, of justification, of glorification, and in every act of God, and in whatever one may say about faith, hope and love, we are, so to speak, invited to take part in this action of God with himself. We are invited to listen to a conversation within the Godhead. No less than that! No longer are we at home. We are at God's place. God himself has opened his arms to us.

It must be hoped that the lack of understanding and the theological ignorance which so many historians and so many "theologians" have demonstrated will be replaced by a fairer understanding of the importance of the early Church's theological disputes (which, to be sure, were not always patterns of Christian affection or intellectual probity . . .). The books on the history of dogma we possess are very scholarly, very thick, but they lack clear-sightedness concerning these questions, simplicity concerning the decisions facing the Church. The criticism leveled against orthodoxy during the past two centuries is quite simply barbarian: it does not even know what it is talking about. Useless complication and subtlety were not shown by those ancient fellows but by the modern savants who did not try to understand and who did not understand.

REMARK II. *On Sin.* Christ's Godhead reveals to us the essence of sin. It must be said that sin was so great, so deep a fault that nothing less than the intervention of God could atone for it. Hence sin consists finally in the refusal of divine grace, even of that grace manifested unto Adam.

IV. OUR LORD

Question 48

QUESTION 48. In what sense do you understand him to be our Lord?—In that he was appointed by the Father to have us under his power, to administer the Kingdom of God in heaven and earth, and to be the head of men and angels.

This explanation is not sufficient. Calvin will hark back to it (Cf. Question 80). The Heidelberg Catechism (34) says on this matter: "Wherefore callest thou Him, our Lord?—Because he hath redeemed us, both soul and body, from all our sins, not with gold or silver, but with His precious blood, and hath delivered us from all the power of the devil; and thus made us His own property." This explanation of the Heidelberg Catechism goes more to the heart because it immediately states how Jesus is our Lord. He not only was established by his Father to the end of having us under his governance. But he did something to be our Lord, and he is our Lord in doing it. We are his property because he has redeemed us, because he has acquired us for himself through his blood, that is, with his life. Therefore, he is our Lord in that he is our Savior.

Our Lord. No compartment of our existence is withdrawn from that Lordship. "Both body and soul," says the Heidelberg Catechism. Hence not only the soul. When you hear tell of the sole mysteries of the inner life, you can be sure that there is flight from the Lordship of Christ. Likewise this Lordship does not restrict itself to the religious realm. It embodies every realm (including the political realm, so important nowadays). Finally, it is very important to stress this "*our* Lord." For we might have understood all about Christology and gone back home to start a general renewal of our lives and our churches to the unanimous admiration of the world. And yet Jesus Christ would not be our Lord, but we would be the lords of Jesus Christ. You all know, I think, this to be the last seduction, the last spiritual peril. We have understood, we are happy, we grasp, we grasp him instead of letting him grasp us, instead of submitting ourselves, instead of obeying. We change the Lord into a human entity of a superior order, to be sure, very superior; but this still always means the Rev. Mr. X and *his* Christianity. And at bottom, that is why we are so unhappy. There we are always with our little Christianities, with various brands of it. We are his advocates instead of his being our Advocate. We intercede for him instead of letting him intercede. We suffer (oh yes! we suffer) but then what about Christ's sufferings? And we are even resurrected; but now a very refined reversal takes place, a very dangerous one with which we delude ourselves concerning our "new lease on life." It is very important that we should reverse everything and learn how to say truly: our Lord, not I, but He, the Lord. And to learn how to live within this continuous quest, the quest of Him who loves me and leads me.

And now something simple enough becomes of primary importance. I mean the reading of the Holy Scripture. Don't you think that the weakness of the Church comes from reading the Bible much too little? We do not let ourselves be led by the Scripture witnessing to Christ. We live on a certain number of ideas, a course in dogmatics and morals. If you're a minister, you preach these things for two or three years. Then you're worn out, and sad, and have nothing more to say because nothing more has been listened to. The same might be said of prayer, for prayer is not an act apart from the Scripture. It is a request really to receive what the Scripture promises.

Jesus Christ, our Lord. This is the secret of the Church's life. And this secret is plainly revealed in the Scripture which leads us day by day, situation after situation, through his Lordship.

V. INTRODUCTION TO QUESTIONS 49-87

Articles 30-48 have taught us that Jesus is the Christ, the Son of God, our Lord. And this is not a theoretical truth, but a fact revealed in a history. Articles 49-87 aim at describing this history and at answering the question: Why, in what sense, is Jesus Christ the only Son of God? How is he our Lord? These articles therefore explain the passage of St. John (1:14): The Word became flesh. For it is through the incarnation that God in Jesus Christ has manifested his Lordship.

The reason for the Christian conviction, according to the Apostles' Creed, cannot then be some general truth of an intellectual, sentimental or even metaphysical order. Rather it is founded upon an event which is the history of Jesus Christ and which manifests the revelation, the propitiation, the establishment of Christ's kingdom, the hope of the kingdom of God.

The life of the whole Church, the life of each particular believer, consists in participation in this history. Participation does not mean mere attendance—as in a theater—or more notation of the facts—as when some remote past is being studied disinterestedly. Rather, by participation we understand that in the history of Jesus Christ our history is being acted; that we "have a part" in his history, a central and decisive part.

Jesus Christ is not the Lord abstractly. His victory is not an ideal victory, nor his forgiveness a logical necessity. But all this, his Lordship, his victory, his forgiveness, is an historical event, something that came to pass and concerns us.

This event comprises three particular moments; the incarnation of the Son of God (Questions 49-54), his exinanition• (Questions 55-72) and his exaltation (Questions 73-87). Or, in other words: his coming in the flesh, his passion, his resurrection. Each of these moments has a particular import, but also each refers to the others so that they explain and imply each other.

VI. DOCTRINE OF THE INCARNATION

Questions 49-54

QUESTIONS 49-54. What is intended by what follows?—It shows the manner in which the Son

---

• Self-emptying, humiliation. Cf. Philippians 2. [Translator]

was anointed by the Father to be our Savior, namely that, assuming our flesh, he performed all things necessary for our salvation, as are here mentioned.

What do you mean by these two phrases, conceived by the Holy Ghost, born of the Virgin Mary?—That he was formed in the womb of a virgin, of her substance, to be the true seed of David, as had been foretold by the predictions of the prophets; and that this was effected by the miraculous and secret agency of the Spirit, without male intercourse (Ps. 132:11; Matt. 1:1, 16; Luke 1:32, 55).

Was it then of importance that he should assume our flesh?—Very much so; because it was necessary that the disobedience committed by man against God be expiated also in human nature (Rom. 5:15). In no other way indeed could he be our mediator to effect reconciliation between God and men (I Tim. 2:5; Heb. 4:14; 5:1).

You say, then, that Christ had to be made man, in order, as in our own person, to fulfil the requirements of our salvation?—That is what I think. For we must obtain from him whatever is lacking in ourselves; and this can be done in no other way.

But why was this effected by the Holy Spirit, and not rather by the common use and form of generation?—Because human seed is wholly corrupt, it was necessary and proper that the Holy Spirit should intervene in the generation of the Son of God, that he might not be affected by this contagion but endued with the most perfect purity.

Thus then we learn that he who sanctifies others is immune from every blemish and endued with purity from the original womb (as one may say), so that he might be entirely sacred to God and infected with no human failing.—I understand the matter so.

Preliminary Remark. Both in the Apostles' Creed and in Calvin's commentary there are two distinctions: a) the mystery of the incarnation, of the union of the logos with the manhood of Jesus; b) the miracle of the virgin birth, sign of that mystery.

These two are related to each other, but they are distinct. It is proper that we now examine under this twofold aspect the words of the Creed "conceived by the Holy Ghost and born of the Virgin Mary" along with Calvin's commentary.

THE MYSTERY OF THE INCARNATION

a) *Conceived by the Holy Ghost*

In the light of the foregoing, "conceived by the Holy Ghost" means that Jesus, in the sense of the Creed and the early Church alike, was God, with no reservation and no ambiguity. In Christ it is God himself who became man, and not a half-god, not an appearance of God. The existence of Jesus is the manifestation of God's existence.

In this connection, Calvin states that the conception by the Holy Ghost was "necessary" to atone for the disobedience man had committed against God. In other words, God alone could allow us to recover in him what we had lost. The phrase "conceived by the Holy Ghost" guarantees the efficacy of God's mercy with regard to mankind and each man in particular.

Moreover, it guarantees the efficacy of revelation. In the New Testament, revelation does not mean God's appearance by means of a being who would be foreign to God, by means of a medium of sorts. Instead it is God's representation by God himself. Nothing or no one is there to play the intermediary between God and man; God himself becomes man. In other words, Jesus Christ not only declares the Covenant between God and man, he is that Covenant. No creature could pretend to make God's Covenant.

The phrase "conceived by the Holy Ghost" therefore prevents any confusion between God and the creature. For, if the creature were capable of representing God, it would somehow participate in his nature. But such is not at all the case, since Jesus Christ is God. In him man and God are not confused, but there is *unity* between the one and the other. As to those men, prophets and apostles, who give witness to Jesus Christ, they do not incarnate God's Covenant, they are not God's Covenant, they simply declare it.

b) *Born of the Virgin Mary*

A while ago we said: it is *God* who becomes man in Jesus Christ. Now we must say: what God becomes in Jesus Christ is *man*. God's existence does not manifest itself otherwise or elsewhere than in this man, Jesus of Nazareth. Calvin rightly insists on this point: it is a question of atoning for our disobedience in our human nature, in us, in the realm we live in. God is no longer remote from us, he does not dispense to us his forgiveness from heaven above, he is quite near us, he is nearer to us than we ourselves are! His manhood is not an appearance (which is the error of docetism), it is real.

A while ago we were insisting on the fact that the phrase "conceived by the Holy Ghost" guaranteed the efficacy of God's mercy unto us. Now it must be remarked that the phrase "born of the Virgin Mary" guarantees the reality of that mercy unto us. God's mercy has reached us in Jesus Christ, God's redemption has been accomplished in our own person. If a while ago we had to note that there is no confusion between God and man in Jesus Christ, now we have to note that there is no separation in him between God and man. For it is in Jesus Christ that we accept God's presence.

The idea (the merely philosophical idea) of a God who remains to be reached, whom we need to seek out because he is absent and remote, has no room in Christian theology. In Jesus Christ, God has sought and found us.

Having said this, we have done nothing but repeated the Christology of the Council of Chalcedon. This Christology—like that of the other early councils—enjoyed no good publicity in the last century. People used to find it complicated, abstract, sometimes useless. But nothing is simpler or more needed: no confusion of God and man in Jesus Christ, and no separation either. Forgetting that there is no confusion we would render God's mercy very problematic. Forgetting that there is no separation we would render it inaccessible to us.

That such reasoning intends to explain what cannot be explained has often been claimed. But we do not pretend to explain and, besides, neither did the Councils nor the Reformers. Like them we want to convey that *event* which is the union, the Covenant, of God and man in Jesus Christ, and which itself is a mystery.

I do not think it could be said that this dogma goes beyond what the New Testament tells us of Christ. Do the Gospels or the Epistles tell us anything other than this: that God was in Christ, that Christ was a man, that we do not have to seek God elsewhere than in him? The dogma of the early councils only throws into relief what the Bible says. It signals two dangers that threaten us each time we read the Bible: either not to recognize that God is in question, or not to recognize that man is in question. It forces us not to leave this straight way. Nor do I see how one can, without this basis in the Christological dogma, understand justification and sanctification as taught by the Reformers.

THE MIRACLE OF THE BIRTH OF JESUS

In the New Testament, a miracle is not merely a marvelous event, a wonder. It is a *sign,* it accompanies the words and explains them, it testifies to their reality.

The same holds here. This word: God become man in Jesus Christ, which we read all through the Bible, is accompanied by a particular sign: the miraculous birth.

We shall now examine the two elements "conceived by the Holy Ghost" and "born of the Virgin Mary" from the point of view of their character as miracle or as sign, and no longer as before, from the point of view of their character as Word.

a) *Conceived by the Holy Ghost*

What does it signify that Jesus Christ was conceived by the Holy Ghost? In no case does it mean that the Holy Spirit was the father of Jesus. There was no wedding between the Holy Spirit and Mary! A Christian of the second century or the third would never have understood or admitted such an interpretation of this passage.

Rather, it signifies quite simply: Jesus Christ has no human father because he is the beginning of a new mankind, or a mankind according to God. This is a new beginning, a new creation, different however from the first creation in that there already was something: there was Mary. This new creation implies and necessitates an *exclusion of human sin* so that what was done wrong through Adam and through us may be done well through the person of Christ. Exclusion of sin, therefore action of the Holy Spirit.

Now in what sense may we say that sin was excluded by this process? Here I can no longer follow the tradition of the early theologians who insisted that sexuality was sinfulness in itself, and had to be excluded! I see nowhere in the Bible, neither in the Old nor in the New Testament, that the sexual realm is the receptacle of sin. Such an interpretation, so characteristic of the Christian milieu, smacks of the cloister, the monks. Sexual asceticism is a pagan and not a biblical idea.

The Bible says nothing else than this: Joseph was not the natural father of Jesus; man, the male, was excluded. Man represents the more glorious aspect of mankind, it is he who conducts business, who makes history, who speaks, thinks, writes. To him was the sovereignty given and he has lost it. God excludes man, the fallen sovereign. For it was he, Adam, who was called a sinner, although in the history of sin the woman played no little role, since she was the first who discussed theology! It is Adam, the glorious man and maker of history, who is deemed improper for God's designs. God steps into the act in Adam's place. Not that he becomes husband to the woman, but through the action of his Holy Spirit he renders Joseph useless.

b) *Born of the Virgin Mary*

What does it *signify* that Jesus was born of the Virgin Mary? In no case does it mean—as Schleiermacher supposed—that the woman in herself had been privileged. Schleiermacher even supposed that woman does not need conversion, that she by nature is closer to God than man is.

Woman, in contradistinction to man, represents the weaker aspect of mankind. Yet the part of mankind chosen by God is the weaker part. Glory is discarded, weakness is accepted. Or again, history is discarded, nature is accepted. Or again: triumphant man is rejected, suffering and serving man is chosen.

In the person of Mary, mankind does then have a part in the incarnation. Not merely passively does mankind play this part, nor triumphantly, but by virtue of its freedom—even that of the weaker creature, of a servant: "Behold I am the handmaid of the Lord; let it be to me according to your word" (Luke 1:38).

This is not a question of merit. Mary is sinful like every woman. Her freedom consists in being able to receive grace, creative of obedience.

REMARK I. *On the Freedom of God in Relation to Miracle.* We have distinguished between miracle and mystery, between sign and the thing signified. Some specification is needed here: the sign does not prove the thing signified, it communicates it. In other words, this miracle was not necessary for the incarnation. God could have chosen another process, even as Jesus could have done other miracles to signify the same Word. Hence the distinction between sign and the thing signified must be maintained.

REMARK II. *On the Necessity of the Miracle Occurring for Our Sake.* What we have just said, by no means entails that we could have the thing signified without the sign. Quite the contrary, there would be the danger that, by eliminating the sign, we thereby eliminate the thing signified. Exactly this seems to have happened to all those who have wanted to get rid of the miraculous birth: they have lost the incarnation along with it. It might even be said that the denial of the virginal conception necessarily entails the abandonment of revealed theology for the sake of natural theology. Conversely, wherever the incarnation and the free grace of Christ's existence as the secret of our union with God are properly understood, it will not be strange to find just this miracle. On the contrary, it would be surprising if it were not there.

It is on this ground—the dogmatic ground—that the question of the miraculous birth must be based. For the various exegetical considerations do not result in any decision.

VII. DOCTRINE OF EXINANITION

Questions 55-72

QUESTION 55. Why do you make the transition forthwith from birth to death, omitting all the story of his life?—Because nothing is dealt with here except what so pertains to our redemption, as in some degree to contain the substance of it.

Here we must make some criticism of Calvin. I contest Calvin's opinion that the Creed has omitted the whole history of the life of Jesus Christ. In the Gospels, the whole history of Jesus is the history of his passion and cross, still more, of his resurrection. By speaking of the passion, cross and resurrection, the Creed recalls the whole substance of the Gospel narratives. As to Calvin's answer, it is decidedly insufficient: the life of Jesus, his miracles, his preaching, his relationship with the apostles, do they not all belong to the substance of redemption? Is all this not full of his passion and full of his resurrection?

HE SUFFERED UNDER PONTIUS PILATE

QUESTIONS 56-59. Why do you not say simply in one word that he died instead of adding also the name of the governor under whom he suffered? —This has reference not only to our credence of the story, but that we may know his death to have been connected with his condemnation. Explain this more clearly.—He died so that the penalty owed by us might be discharged, and he might exempt us from it. But since we all, because we are sinners, were offensive to the judgment of God, in order to stand in our stead, he desired to be arraigned before an earthly judge, and to be condemned by his mouth, so that we might be acquitted before the heavenly tribunal of God.

But Pilate pronounces him innocent (Matt. 27:23; Luke 23:14), and hence does not condemn him as malefactor.—Both things must be considered. For the judge bears testimony to his innocence, so that there may be evidence that he suffered not for his own misdeeds but for ours. Nevertheless, at the same time he is formally condemned by the same judge to make it plain that he suffered as our surety the judgment which we deserved, that thus he might free us from guilt.

Well said. For if he were a sinner, he would not be a fit surety to pay the penalty of another's sin. Nevertheless, that his condemnation might secure our acquittal, it was requisite that he be reckoned among the malefactors (Isa. 53:12).— So I understand it.

The Son of God, become man in his unity with man, could do nothing else than suffer in the situation of man. God and man meet. This necessarily means conflict. From the beginning we see in the history of Jesus that he is a stranger among men, is disregarded and despised, and that men are hostile to him. This hostility unceasingly grows worse until the cross. But it is not like the suffering known by a misunderstood genius, it partakes of a much higher necessity: it manifests the opposition between God and man which breaks out in him who was at once God and man. On the one hand it shows God's wrath against men, on the other hand it shows men's revolt against God. The suffering of Jesus makes manifest the real origin of this opposition, that is, sin.

Through the total suffering of Jesus, the total sin which is its cause breaks out. Thus Jesus alone knows the totality of suffering. Man thrown into the conflict of his existence, into the impossibility of living, into the abyss of solitude, of war, and finally of death and hell, is disclosed through the person of him who was God and man in his own person. But not every man suffers such total suffering: Jesus Christ alone does. We believe we know suffering, conflict, sorrow, death. The truth is we only know vague glimpses of them. To suffer what man should suffer because he is God's enemy would mean our annihilation. Precisely here, God's mercy bursts out: it is God himself who in the person of his son suffered that very total suffering. God himself, in Jesus Christ, offers himself to man in order to bear, as representative of mankind, the suffering that man had to suffer.

We now see that Christ's incarnation was the beginning of his suffering, that the incarnation as such is Christ's suffering since through it he takes our place. The incarnation as such is exinanition: from the very beginning Jesus is suffering. The stable, Herod's persecution, the flight into Egypt are its signs. What Christ suffered under Pontius Pilate is but the solemn declaration of the condemnation pronounced by the divine wrath.

Calvin, following the Creed, insists on the presence of Pontius Pilate. He sees in Pilate first of all an historical reference intended to accredit the passion narrative. But especially, Calvin wants to point out that the world par excellence, the authority of the world which Pilate represented, can do nothing but make Jesus suffer. Thus it is that the sin of the world breaks forth. But thus it is that God's mercy also breaks forth. For Jesus is seen suffering *in our place*. In a way, then, Pilate fulfils the New Testament: he declares Jesus innocent and, nevertheless, finally works his condemnation. Our condemnation is thus eliminated.

Christ's suffering necessarily signifies that the Godhead of Christ (as Calvin somewhere says) is hidden under the contrary appearance. No less was needed for God to take upon himself our suffering. And now he has taken it. "Behold the man." Behold man in whose place God has put himself. Behold his condemnation, behold his suffering, behold what we deserve!

Still to be explained is the relationship between suffering and victory in the cross of Jesus Christ. All along the line, these are the two moments: suffering and victory. Not only has Jesus *taken on* our suffering, he has also *taken* it *away*. The message of the cross is not only the message of sorrow and defeat, but even at the same time it is the message of victory and resurrection. If not, it would have no meaning. There is no absolute distinction between the message of Good Friday and that of Easter. For Easter is understood only through Good Friday, and Good Friday only in Easter.

HE WAS CRUCIFIED

> QUESTIONS 60-61. Is the fact that he was crucified
> of greater importance than if he suffered any
> other kind of death?—Certainly, as even Paul
> reminds us (Gal. 3:10), when he writes that he
> hung upon the tree to take our curse upon him-
> self; and by this we are absolved from it. For
> this kind of death was regarded with execration
> (Deut. 21:23).
> What? Is it not to offer an affront to the Son
> of God to say that he was subject to a curse,
> even before God?—Not at all; for by undergo-
> ing it he abolished it. Nor does he meanwhile
> cease to be blessed, in order that he bestow his
> blessing on us.

This article and the following ones aim at completely describing the central word: suffered.
Hence they must equally be seen from the view-
point: he rose again.

"He was crucified." Behold man in the light of
God: a cursed one. But this cursed one is God himself who, in Jesus Christ, accepts so to be. God
condemned sin in the flesh (Rom. 8:3), not in our
own flesh but in that of Jesus Christ. And by accepting the curse of his flesh, Jesus Christ annihi-
lated that curse. There no longer exists any object
under the curse after what happened on Calvary.
By taking over that curse Christ accomplished our
acquittal. Here again, as above, taking on, taking
over and taking away go together.

HE WAS DEAD

> QUESTIONS 62-64. Go on.—Since death was the
> punishment imposed on man because of his sin,
> the Son of God endured it, and by enduring
> conquered it. But that it might better appear
> that he suffered real death, he desired to be laid
> in the tomb, just like other men.
>
> But we seem to gain nothing from this victory,
> since we still have to die.—That is no obstacle.
> For death for believers is now nothing but the
> passage to a better life.
>
> Hence it follows that death is no longer to be
> dreaded, as if it were a fearful thing. We are
> rather to follow Christ our leader with un-
> daunted mind, who, as he did not perish in
> death, will not suffer us to perish?—We should
> do so.

According to Rom. 6:23, the wages of sin is
death. The sinful man cannot subsist before God,
he dies. On entering into this consequence of sin,
Jesus Christ dies in our place. He endures and
overcomes death. He accepts our impossibility of
living. And, in the same way, he abolishes the impossibility of our life.

This is that reality of which the sacrifices of the
Old Covenant were only a figure. In order that life
may be available to man, there must be death elsewhere. But how could an animal sacrifice have any
efficacy? It was only a figure of the sacrifice of Jesus
Christ. Death is virtually overcome for our sake.

You perhaps know the illustration used by a
Greek Father: Death, figured by an enormous

beast, seizes the Christ. But it itself dies in fighting against him. In overcoming the Christ, death is overcome by him.

HE WAS BURIED

It is interesting to note that the Creed found it necessary to speak of the burial. In this it only follows the New Testament (I Cor. 15). Man is not yet quite dead either before he is left alone in his tomb, or after the rest of the people have gone away. The Christ also, Christ first of all and chiefly, knew that solitude of the tomb. But this end is not "the" end. For him it is passage only. And consequently for us too it is just a passage.

HE DESCENDED INTO HELL

QUESTIONS 65-70. As for what immediately follows, that he descended into hell, what does this mean?—That he endured not only common death, which is the separation of the soul from the body; but also the pains of death, as Peter calls them (Acts 2:24). By this word I understand the fearful agonies with which his soul was tormented.

Tell me the cause and manner of this.—Because, in order to make satisfaction for sinners, he arraigned himself before the tribunal of God, it was requisite that his conscience be tormented by such agony as if he were forsaken by God, even as if he had God hostile to him. He was in this agony, when he cried to the Father: "My

God, my God, why hast thou forsaken me?"
(Matt. 27:46; Mark 15:34).

Was this not an affront to the Father?—Not at
all. But he exercised this severity against him,
that he might fulfil what was prophesied by
Isaiah: He was smitten by the hand of God for
our sins, wounded for our iniquities (Isa. 53:4;
I Pet. 2:24).

But since he is God, how could he be seized
by fear of this kind, as if he were forsaken of
God?—We must hold him to have been reduced
to this necessity in respect of the feelings of his
human nature. That this might happen, his
divinity was for a short while concealed, that is,
it did not exercise its power. Yet on the other
hand, how can it be that Christ who is the salvation of the world should have been subjected
to this condemnation?—He did not so endure it
as to remain under it. For he was so seized by
those fears I have mentioned as not to be over-
whelmed. Rather, contending with infernal
might, he subdued and broke it.

Hence we conclude that the torment of conscience he endured differed from that which
torments sinners, whom the hand of an angry
God pursues. For what was temporary in his case
is perpetual in theirs; and what was for him
like a prick stinging him is for them a mortal
sword wounding, as one may say, the very heart.
—Just so. For the Son of God, though beset by
agonies of this kind, did not cease to hope in
the Father. But sinners, condemned by God's
judgment, rush into despair, rage against him,
and break forth even into open blasphemies.

Calvin interpreted the descent into hell in the
light of these words of Christ on the cross: My

God, my God, why hast thou forsaken me? The descent into hell deals with Jesus Christ cast into despair, into distress of conscience, into that feeling that God is against him. The descent into hell is, so to speak, the inward explanation of what is outwardly happening in his death and tomb. As soon as the body is buried, the soul goes to hell, that is, into remoteness from God, into that place where God can only be the Adversary, the enemy. In our place the Christ suffered that situation which ought to have been ours. Our lives too know despair. But it is not, it is no longer, that total despair suffered by Jesus Christ alone.

This distinction between the Christ and us ought to keep us from dramatizing our sorrows, however grievous they might be. For we now know that Jesus Christ has destroyed the power of hell, however great it may be.

THE FRUIT OF CHRIST'S DEATH

QUESTIONS 71-72. Can we infer from this what benefit the faithful obtain from the death of Christ? —Certainly. For a beginning, we see it to be a sacrifice by which he expiates our sins in the sight of God, and so appeases the wrath of God and restores us to grace with him. Then, too, his blood is a laver in which our souls are purged of every stain. Lastly, the memory of our sins is erased, so that they never come before God; and thus the handwriting by which we were declared guilty is canceled and abolished.

Does it not offer us any other advantage besides? —Yes, indeed. For by his benefit, if we are true members of Christ, our old nature is crucified, and the body of sin is destroyed, so that the lusts of perverse flesh no longer rule in us.

Calvin's statements with regard to the passion definitely forbid any tragic view of man's situation. We are not in the situation of men who themselves need to fight against evil. This fight *is accomplished*, "all is accomplished." Do not make Good Friday into a mournful and sinister thing. But make it what it is: Jesus Christ has taken over and taken away our human distress. It is really pitiful that it is precisely the Christians who are oftentimes the biggest "grumblers" against the miseries of the world, whereas they should know that these are taken over and taken away by Jesus Christ and that they should live on this faith. We can, we ought to be Christian in another way: by living on this great Yes that God said in the cross of Jesus Christ. Yes, our human life is now possible.

VII. DOCTRINE OF THE EXALTATION

Questions 73-87

PRELIMINARY REMARKS

REMARK I. *On the Christological Notion of History.* We have already seen (Cf. Introduction to the second article) that Calvin, in keeping with the Creed, invites us to follow the unfolding of Christ's history in the past movement of his life, death, resurrection, ascension, and in the present movement of his kingship on the right hand of God, and in the future movement of his return and judgment. When we attend the making of this history, we understand what Jesus Christ is. And when we repeat the words, "I believe," which introduce the Creed, we affirm our participation in that history and we confess that we are figures drawn into involvement in that history. The history of Jesus Christ, precisely, that is my history! It is closer to me than the various events of my own life. It is most important that this point be fully understood. The history of Christ is not an explanation of my life and the life of the Church, *after the event*. It is not one possible idea thanks to which my life may be given a certain interpretation. It is not a revelation of a certain number of abstract truths that may fortunately apply to the life of the Christian and of the Church. No! Rather, it constitutes the very history both of the Christian and of the Church. This is what the Church means when she confesses her faith: she has heard the apostles' message, the testimony of those who attended Christ's history. And facing that history, the only "interesting story" ever to have occurred. This history thus points beyond the Church. It is the background and the secret reality of all mankind and even of every creature. In the world what characterizes and locates the Church is that the Church acknowledges this history and confesses it as *the* history par excellence, the unique history. The Church is wherever this history is so acknowledged and confessed, and there only is the Church.

In summing up what the Creed tells I used the term "history." It is important to understand this term without prejudice. Of ourselves, as would-be modern men, we indulge in a certain representation of history along the lines of some coherence of events in time, according to our grasp of them. Our reason and our experience allow us a representation of the past and this forms our "historical sense." But it must be realized that our understanding of history is not necessarily objective. It has its use, though a relative and at times problematic use. Here in this room for instance look at Farel's or Osterwald's portraits. In order to understand these historical characters, still more is needed than a study of their actions or of historical sources. A certain flair for what happened, for what they wanted, did and left undone, is necessary. Moreover, without faith, they may perhaps never be understood; nor for that matter the battle of Waterloo or contemporary history. For secrets and mysteries persist in any occurrence, secrets and mysteries that escape any purely scientific apprehension even though accompanied by historical flair. This is why the affirmations of the Creed are not to be submitted to a ready-made conception of history. To do so would be like someone who wants to see with his eyes shut. We must open our eyes and see this quite particular history: God becomes man, the Word was made flesh, it lived in the midst of men. Thus not only is there a history other than our human history with its pains and joys, its battles and treaties, its inventions and events, but there is also another definition of history. By this definition the decisive events seem to be located elsewhere than where we ourselves would locate them.

The articles which we shall deal with, concerning the resurrection, the ascension, and the return of Christ, might be qualified as "nonhistorical" and mythical by men who would judge according to men's notion of history. Why not classify them in the same sequence with the miraculous narratives of every people on the earth? Why not treat them like those of Jewish apocalyptics? Strangely enough, it must be observed that neither Jews nor pagans have been mistaken. They have not embraced the Christian "myth." On the contrary, they have rejected it with the utmost violence. The reason is that this "myth" does not fit in the framework of the others. One must choose then between this myth and the others. Or, rather, one must clearly either accept this "myth" as history itself, and call all the other histories myth, or otherwise refuse the Christian "myth" and remain with the human notion of history.

The Christian Church confesses that this "myth" is history itself. She recognizes herself by this myth, she recognizes her life, her true reality. She is the witness of witnesses, she recognizes through the Holy Spirit that this is the only really interesting story. Thus she turns back the historians' weapon: she says to them: What you call "myth," that is history! She will add also: What you call history, that is a myth! A myth, a made-up history, what fancies the fate of man as depending on his earthly vicissitudes, a myth, a made-up history, what confuses the immediate success of a cause with its truth, and so on. The only true history is the history of Christ, in which the Church participates, and which is already the secret reality of all history, since it is history itself.

REMARK II. *On God's Almightiness, the Only Master of the Exinanition and Exaltation of Christ, and on Their Connections.* It is not possible to know how to deduce the necessity of a Savior from the preliminary statement that we are lost. Likewise, we cannot infer the resurrection from the cross, by means of some kind of immanental logic. In both cases, exinanition and exaltation, it is a question of a deed by the power of God who lowers himself in Jesus Christ until death and even until the death on the cross; and who triumphs by the resurrection of that same Jesus Christ. Neither exinanition nor exaltation are abstract philosophical truths which we might draw from a more general truth accessible as such to our knowledge. Christ's resurrection does not follow his death as morning follows evening, as spring follows winter, and as good days come again after bad days. It is not a consequence independent of the active will of God. Unfortunately, that is how we often interpret Easter: we fancy, we invent, some kind of life after death, after the tragedy of Good Friday, we say: Yes, in spite of it all, truth will triumph. We put ourselves into a certain state of enthusiasm, we almost wish to encourage the good Lord or at least ourselves and our parishioners . . . All of you have already preached some of those Easter sermons in which you hold your breath to emphasize life, spirit, victory, have you not? And try as you would to prod yourselves, you were still marking time because you wanted to give yourselves the excitement. But the "excitement" of Easter cannot be given to man by man himself. Even more than his exinanition, Christ's exaltation is the consequence reached by God himself through his power in action. God himself is the rector and the master and the king of this whole history which is his Covenant with us. Either we understand God as master and subject of this history, or we do not understand this history at all. Thus the question we have to answer now is not: "Can I admit that all this occurred?" but: "Where do I stand vis-à-vis God the master? Do I live 'with' God? Do I live in keeping with God's deeds?" And since we know these deeds mainly and primarily through the Scripture, the question of faith is first a question of reading the Bible. One cannot pray without reading the Bible, without getting a knowledge of the divine history directed by God wherein we discover what we need: faith in God the rector and sovereign and living master of Christ's history which "comprehends," that is, embodies, sums up, locates and fulfills our own history.

THE RESURRECTION

Questions 73-74

QUESTION 74. What are the manifold benefits that come to us from his resurrection?—Three. For by it righteousness is obtained for us (Rom. 4:24); it is a sure pledge of our future immortality (I Cor. 15); and even now by its virtue we are raised to newness of life, that we may obey God's will by pure and holy living (Rom. 6:4).

We begin with this question which shows us the fruits of the resurrection. There are three:

1. *Our justification is acquired.* Our justification is not a possession we might have by external right. It must be acquired. Moreover, it must be acquired not by us but on our behalf. The Christ acquires it for us. It is the resurrection that sets us in conformity with the will of God.

2. *The resurrection is a sure pledge that we shall one day rise again for a glorious immortality.* This life come to its end is not vain, it does not fall back into nothingness. It is called to rise again. But the same holds here as in our justification. Both are acquired for us through the resurrection of Christ who is the only pledge, but the sufficient pledge. Every human claim to immortality would be an illusion without this God-given pledge through Christ's resurrection.

3. *If we really participate in Christ's resurrection, we even now rise again in newness of life to serve God and live in holiness, according to his will.* Right now the resurrection assures us a new life that does not belong to us any more than our justification and our resurrection to come. A life lived in the service of God, in holiness, and according to his pleasure—consequently also to our own pleasure. A life of joy because it is a life of service. A life already actual because Christ is already risen and because in him already rests our new life.

In order to understand Calvin's explanation well (I believe he is faithful to the Creed and to the

New Testament), all of these expressions: "Righteousness (i.e., justification) is obtained for us, we shall rise again—and rise even now," must above all be interpreted realistically. The fruits of the resurrection are not desires, hopes, inner feelings: they are facts. Only then is the importance of the resurrection of Christ—the origin and pledge of our own—better understood. Saint Paul, I Cor. 15, says so in two passages: "If there be no resurrection of the dead, then is Christ not risen" (v. 13 and 16). In other words, whoever does not understand the reality of the justification, of the resurrection, of the new life acquired for him through Christ's resurrection has no need of Christ's resurrection. This is why we have begun with Question 74. Indeed the whole reality of the matter is in Christ, but it is important to see from the beginning that we are within his history, that we are the branches of the vine, that we are the members of his body.

Finally note that the fruits of Christ's resurrection are substantially the same as those of his death. (Compare Question 74 with Questions 71-72 and Questions 62-64.) Hence the resurrection is nothing else than the revelation of what Christ's death brings us; the exaltation reveals to us the meaning, the end and the import of his humiliation.

QUESTION 73. Proceed with the remaining articles. —There follows: the third day he rose again from the dead. By this he shows himself to be conqueror over sin and death. For by his resurrection he swallowed up death, broke the fetters of the devil, and reduced all his power to nothing (I Pet. 3:18).

This article properly gives us the explanation and the description of the foundation of our faith in our justification, in our resurrection and in our new life. Once again we must insist on the fact that we are not dealing with illustrations, or with exaggerations of some religious enthusiasm. If it is said: he has overcome and swallowed death, broken the chains of the devil and destroyed his power, this is so: it is done with, it is accomplished. After Christ's resurrection death is no more, nor does sin rule. Indeed death and sin continue to exist, but as vanquished things. Their situation is similar to a chess player's who has already lost but has not acknowledged it as yet. He looks on the game, and he says: Is it already finished? Does the king still have another move? He tries it. Afterwards he acknowledges there was no more possibility of winning. That precisely is the situation of death and sin and the devil: the king is checkmated, the game is finished and the players do not acknowledge it as yet. They still believe the game will go on. But it is over. The old "aeon," the old time of death and sin is over, and the game only appears somehow to be going on. "Old things are passed away; behold, all things are become new" (II Cor. 5:17).

You must note this down: you take it or leave it. Such is Easter, or it is nothing at all. You might say: at bottom nothing has changed since Easter, people die, they fight each other and sin, the devil works as before. But in the light of Easter this idea reveals itself as the grand illusion, the sad human illusion. You should at least realize the falsehood of this idea, of this myth, as previously (Cf. Preliminary Remark I) we called any history independent of Christ's central history. In this case the myth is the belief that still views death and sin as definitely victorious powers. No, that is not true, the demon's chains have been broken. This is the truth. And if we do not admit it, at least let us acknowledge that it is the fault of our eyes which do not see, of our ears which do not hear well, and of our imagination which replaces God's reality with sad illusions. Alone with ourselves we would fancy that the Creed's declarations are the product of enthusiasm, while we and our earthly wisdom are the true realists who know life, evil, and death too. Well, just the opposite is true. We are the enthusiasts, we and our pessimism, our weakness, our false respect for the devil. That is the message of Easter. The important thing for the minister is that he himself believes it above all. It would not be difficult to preach it, if he believed it himself.

Easter inaugurates a new time, but not a new springtime. For a summer and a fall and a winter will follow spring one time or another, whereas in this case occurs an absolute beginning, valid for the whole world, but as yet acknowledged by the Church alone. The time Easter inaugurates is thus the time of the Church: the time that God leaves us, in his great patience, so that we may think and understand and believe; the time that God leaves men so that they may acknowledge and receive his victory.

"He shows himself to be conqueror over death." Jesus Christ is the subject of resurrection. He himself showed he was victor, and his victory grounds our faith. It is not our faith that grounds his victory. The idea of a faith triumphant over death must be avoided. Indeed, it is said: Our faith overcomes the world. But this is so because our faith is

in him. We would never find ourselves the strength, not to mention the "faith," needed to assert the resurrection. Or else it would be the enthusiastic expression of an impotent illusion! Faith is not an idea about God, it is the consequence in man of the action of God himself.

"He rose again." There are two elements in the term "to rise again": to awake after having slept; to rise up after having lain down. In sleep, we are, so to speak, outside ourselves, we do not control our persons. We find ourselves in the unconscious, in dreams, as if in the hands of another power. On awaking, on "rising," we reenter life. This is the formal sense of the word resurrection. But this still is an image of the resurrection. For each of us who rises up will again lie down, and at the end of our lives, every one of us will lie down. Our uprisings are but little images of the great and only uprising of Christ in his resurrection. We begin in our mother's bosom, and we end up in the bosom of the earth. But there is always this little image: a man rising up, trying to live. But it is a try only. Christ's resurrection, on the contrary, is the resurrection par excellence: Christ rose up out of death, he lives, he stands up, he watches, as God himself rises up, without setback, without relapse. There, in the Christ risen, lies the truly human reality.

The New Testament describes Easter by two assertions: the women found the tomb empty, then they met the risen Christ acting in their midst in a humanly-speaking very strange and new yet very real manner. The mention of the empty tomb in the Gospels irrefutably marks the bodily resurrection. By this, we are instructed concerning man and his life: he is body and spirit. When he is living, he lives as body and soul. Hence also man's resurrection necessarily is corporeal.

It may be said: this is impossible. A dead man does not reenter life. It never happened. It is even a contradiction in terms. Death means: life has ended, and it cannot be started again. One would be then facing the dilemma: Either the Christ died and did not rise again, or he rose again and was not dead. Schleiermacher was always posing this dilemma and stopping at the second possibility. For him the death of Jesus was just an appearance. Jesus had been in stupor. Then he was buried without being dead, which always is very sad as a German pastor remarked in his sermon, inferring from this regrettable story the necessity of not burying the dead too quickly . . . But all this has nothing to do with Christ's resurrection in the New Testament.

The New Testament is much simpler than that. It tells us quite simply: Do you want to believe in the living Christ? And it shows us that we may believe in him only if we believe in his corporeal resurrection. For life without a body is not human life. This is the content of the New Testament. We are always free to reject it, but not to modify it nor to pretend that the New Testament tells something else. We may accept or refuse the message, but we may not change it. Besides, no one is compelled to believe it. But it would be sad if Theology were trying to facilitate things and invent a Christianity without Christ's resurrection. And if we should find it difficult to believe, rather than modifying the message let us pray God that he give us faith, through his Holy Spirit.

REMARK *on the "Historicity" of the Resurrection.*
Unquestionably, the resurrection narratives are
contradictory. A coherent history cannot be
evolved from them. The appearances to the women
and apostles, in Galilee and Jerusalem, which are
reported by the Gospels and Paul, cannot be har-
monized. It is a chaos. The evangelical theologians
of the nineteenth century—my father, for instance
—were wrong in trying to arrange things so as to
prove the historicity of the resurrection. Their intention deserved praise. But they should have remembered that even the early Church had not
tried to harmonize the resurrection stories. She had
really felt that about this unique event there was
something of an earthquake for everybody in attendance. The witnesses attended an event that
went over their heads, and each told a bit of it.
But these scraps are sufficient to bear witness to us
of the magnitude of the event and its historicity.
Every one of the witnesses declares God's free grace
which surpasses all human understanding. God
alone can prove the truth of that history since he
himself is its subject. Fortunately, God has never
ceased to work in men's hearts and send the faith
needed to see those things.

THE ASCENSION

Questions 75-82

As we did when we explained the resurrection,
we begin with the fruit of the Ascension: "he sitteth on the right hand of God."

QUESTIONS 80-82. In what sense do you say that he sits at the right hand of the Father?—These words mean that the Father conferred on him the dominion of heaven and earth, so that he rules all things (Matt. 28:18).

But what is meant by the right hand, and what by his sitting?—It is a metaphor taken from princes, who are wont to place at their right hand those whom they make their vicegerents. You mean, then, nothing but what Paul says, namely, that Christ is constituted head of the Church (Eph. 1:21), and raised above all principalities, and given a name which is above every name.—Just as you say (Phil. 2:9).

The expression "right hand of God" does not designate a place, but a function, that of God's lieutenant, the sovereign's minister. Christ holds in his hands the power of God. He governs in God's name. Or again: God's power has become his. There is no divine almightiness without Jesus Christ. To declare that God governs the world amounts to saying: Jesus Christ governs the world. The power revealed in the reconciliation of the cross, in the forgiveness of sins, in the act of divine justice and mercy, is identical with the power of the "God Almighty" over the whole world, mentioned significantly at this point of the Creed. Here we see concretely how the first article (on God the Father and on creation) must be understood. Here we are shown God's power in its exact and concrete manifestation: Christ's power. We also learn that, even as there is no division of power—between "creating" power and "redeeming" power, between the power of "justice" and the power of "love"—so there is no division of realms between a political and an ecclesiastical realm, between a scientific or artistic one and a "religious" realm. Nothing is severed from this divine power which is the power of Christ. And this power of Christ creates only one realm, one dominion embodying the totality of creation.

The divine power is in the hands of Jesus Christ. Question 82 divides and develops this truth in two assertions: "He was constituted head of the Church" and "He was raised above all principalities and given a name which is above every name."

He was constituted head of the Church. Thus, in the Church there lies no other power than his. When we speak of the government of the Church, we should speak clearly and say that any Church government, ministers, session, synod or bishop, are just vice-governments. No human government may be the effective government. But each human government may only bear witness to the real government, and has a right to its authority only to the extent in which it serves God in Jesus Christ. Now appears the great—and perhaps, after all, the sole —question we have to address to the Roman Church: to what extent is the pope's infallibility not competing with that of Jesus Christ? To what extent does the authority of the church not take the place of that of Jesus Christ?

He was raised above all principalities, and given a name which is above every name. There are principalities in the world, powers in nature and history. The dominion of Christ is not without connections with these. Christ was exalted above them. He rules not only over the Church, but also over all creation, even if creation ignores it. Recently, this notion has been taken up and illuminated on many points by my colleague Cullmann in his work on *La royaute de Christ et l'église dans le Nouveau Testament.*• Every man is under the dominion of Christ, whether he knows it or does not know it. On the whole, the Christ is not a novelty for the pagan. Of his own Lord the pagan hears as he listens to the missionary. The difference between the Church and the world is that in the Church the Lord of the world is acknowledged and confessed, whereas in the world he is still ignored. But the same Lord rules over both.

> QUESTIONS 75-79. We go on to the rest.—He ascended into heaven.
> But did he so ascend as to be no longer on earth?—Just so. For after he had performed all things enjoined him by the Father and pertaining to our salvation, there was no need for him to continue longer on earth.
> What good do we obtain from the ascension?—There is a double benefit. For since Christ is entered into heaven in our name, as he had descended to earth for our sakes, he opens up for us a way there; so that the gate is now open to us which was formerly closed on account of sin (Rom. 8:34). Then, too, he appears before God as intercessor and advocate on our behalf (Heb. 7:25).
> But did Christ in taking himself to heaven withdraw from us so that now he has ceased to

---

• *Cahier biblique de Foi et Vie,* Paris 1941. (The Kingship of Christ and the Church in the New Testament.)

be with us?—Not at all. On the contrary, he has
undertaken to be with us even to the end of the
world (Matt. 28:20).

But when he is said to dwell with us, does this
mean that he is bodily present?—No. There is
on the one hand the body received up into
heaven (Luke 24:51; Acts 1:9); and there is on
the other his virtue which is diffused everywhere.

In the New Testament, the fact of Jesus' ascension is not as clearly indicated as his resurrection.
Some Gospels, it seems, do not even distinguish it
from the resurrection; in other passages it is pre-
supposed but not mentioned: the reigning Christ
is spoken of but there is no indication that he
ascended into heaven. In the Creed, the ascension
appears to be one of the main facts of Christ's history. However, against the background of the New
Testament, what is the meaning of ascension
stressed as a fact by the Creed? I think that the
significance of the ascension among the appearances of the Risen One is that it specifically reveals that his power is divine. Jesus Christ is not
only risen, but is risen as Son of God. Calvin says:
as lieutenant of God. The Risen One is not only
saved from death. He has entered into possession
of almightiness.

"The door is now open to us, which had been
closed on account of our sins." In sum, the ascension reveals the ultimate truth of God's Covenant.
Man is enabled to live within this Covenant from
which nothing will separate him since his Savior's
power is now almighty.

The ascension is thus the last of Christ's appearances. With it ceases the earthquake we spoke of,

and a new time begins: the time in which Christ reigns, in which God already showed his victory, but in which this victory is not yet manifested. Man can now live in the light of God's love. Yet he lives with all his human weakness, still subjected to death. His history goes on like the chess game with which we compared it: it is over, but still he must acknowledge this during the time of awaiting—which is also the time of God's patience —which is the time granted him before the victory is gloriously and ultimately manifested. The ascension inaugurates the time of awaiting, the time of the Church. In the Scripture, this time is qualified as very short, and we had better realize that it is very short indeed. It is short not because it might run away fast and give us the impression of a stream of oblivion and destruction, but because it is not characterized by autonomy or fixity. It has simply been left to us, lent to us, that we may believe, make penitence and profit by God's patience for our good. God does not want to conclude history without our presence in that accomplishment, through faith. He does not want to conclude it before the cry, the call, the proclamation, the invitation of the Gospel have been spread over the world. God permits that there still be newer generations, born in the years of grace of this world, which in a way has already come to an end, and who only need to acknowledge it.

The ascension consists of still another element of realism that may not be left out; and any too eager interpretation of it would be dangerous. People have often made fun of this idea of "ascending into heaven." They have asked whether Christ did it like some kind of bird or aviator. And, later on, they have objected that the astronomical heaven is not God's abode, that heaven is at the nadir quite as much as at the zenith, and that the ascension should be interpreted in a merely "spiritual" sense. We must be cautious. I would not advise anyone to deny this movement from the bottom up. It is not just an illustration. On the contrary, it deals with quite a movement from the bottom up, a change of place. Of course, we must understand, the place to which Christ goes, this "right hand of God," is a divine place. There is a divine place as there is a divine time. Place and time are not qualities of the creature only. There is a divine time, and a place, and God is the origin of time and place, as he is of every reality. Thus, when we speak of "God's right hand," we must understand the true and real government of God's right hand. The eyes, the hands of God the Scripture speaks of are not simply images. It is God who has the real eyes and the real hands, the "prime" eyes and the "prime" hands. All we know, our human eyes, our human hands, our various human places, are but secondary. The creature displays something of an image of God's reality. The same holds for the Ascension: he has ascended, he has changed his place. Yes, he has changed his place. And if someone should accept, all in one piece, what he learned in Sunday School, I should tell him: you are wiser than if you were to interpret the ascension in a merely spiritualistic sense!

There is then a change of place, a movement "from bottom up," undoubtedly not a movement from the ground up into the clouds, but a movement from the human place to the divine place.

The essential thing of the ascension is this movement with its direction. Christ was revealed as he who is in the divine place. Indeed, it was not at that moment that he went up above, since he was always there. But it was at that moment that he appeared as he who is above. A preacher of the Gospel should always show this movement: from bottom up! It is part of Christ's truth. It refutes all attempts at setting up another government, another "place," from where orders and promises would reach us. It is the ultimate refutation of all dictatorships.

THE RETURN OF CHRIST AND THE JUDGMENT

Questions 83-87

QUESTIONS 83-85. We go on to other things.—From thence he will come to judge both the quick and the dead. The meaning of these words is that he will come openly to judge the world, just as he was seen to ascend (Acts 1:11).

Since the day of judgment is not before the end of the world, how do you say that there will be some men still alive, when it is appointed to all men once to die? (Heb. 9:27).—Paul answers this question when he says that they who survive will pass into a new state by a sudden change, so that, the corruption of the flesh being abolished, they will put on incorruption (I Cor. 15:52; I Thess. 4:17).

Then you understand this change to be like death for them, that there will be an abolition of the first nature and the beginning of a new? —That is what I mean.

First of all let us note the change of tense: until now we have had assertions about the past: he was dead, he rose again, etc. Now we deal with a future event: from thence he will come to judge the living and the dead. By virtue of the fact that Christ is with the Father, as his lieutenant, all this "past perfect" becomes future. What is past is not simply a past event: it is a "perfect." It is accomplished and what is accomplished cannot be a reality if at the same time it does not determine and shape what is to come. Thus our time is "beset behind and before" by God's time. Not only do we come from God, but we go to him. This is the essential meaning of New Testament Christian eschatology: a new conception of time. The newness of time is not simply a change of tenses: it is the actual fulfillment of the "perfect" which fills and determines the future. Our awaiting is then not an illusion: it is founded on the "perfect," on the "accomplished," and this is a hope that will not be mistaken. Our future and our present are founded on the "perfect" which God has given us in Christ: it is given us not only in the act of faith through which we approach him who has accomplished all and will accomplish everything.

In Question 83, it is said: "From thence he will come to judge the quick and the dead." In other words, he will bring forth a judgment from heaven, he comes on behalf of God. Christ's history—our real history—is divine in its conclusion as well as in its beginning. Christ shall come to us. It is not up to us to seek him out. God's free grace shall thus manifest itself until the end, and we will not escape from it. His work shall confirm itself.

As to the judgment (Question 84), we must consider that the sense of this word is objective. Judgment means: to establish, to set up, to proclaim the lawful right. This entails two consequences: a ruling on men, some of whom will be acquitted, others condemned. But also and first: the establishment of order in the world, the public and irrefutable and victorious proclamation of the truth. In our world and time, the Gospel is proclaimed, death is overcome. But we still live as if all that had not been clarified. Good and evil, justice and injustice, seemingly amount to the same for us. But this false belief shall be refuted definitively. Publicly and irrefutably, the judge shall declare what is just, and everyone shall see it.

This judgment shall be pronounced on the living and the dead, that is, on men of all times. It will not be just any event, one historical event, nor even the last of historical events. It will be the event par excellence, the disclosure of the whole perfect truth accomplished in Christ, the judgment of all men and every one of their lives. It is interesting to note that Calvin, who was still enough of a lawyer, did not speak of this judgment in strictly juridical terms, but presented the last judgment right off from the much broader angle of the manifestation of the truth.

QUESTIONS 86-87. Does it give any happiness to our conscience to know that Christ will one day judge the world?—Indeed, a quite peculiar happiness. For we know that he will come for our salvation only.

Then it is not proper that we should dread this judgment as though it struck terror in us?—No,

indeed, since we shall stand only at the tribunal
of a judge who is also our advocate, and who has
taken us into his faithful protection.

Did Calvin, a somber and angry man as some
imagine him, borrow from his age this graceful
representation of the judgment? He did not! He
interpreted the Scripture. In his time and before,
people endeavored to present the last judgment
under the most horrible colors. Think of Michelangelo's *Last Judgment*: a Christ coming back and
holding out his fist! As you know, it is below that
painting that many popes were elected! But this
is not the Christian notion of Christ's return,
which is all comfort, because our judge is our advocate at the same time. We have no reason to fear
him nor to hold him in horror. To fear the last
judgment is a pagan (Persian, for instance), not a
Christian idea. There is only one who might be
against us: Jesus Christ. And it is he, precisely, who
is for us! God's children know well that they are
unworthy of it, that they live in a very deplorable
state, but insofar as they let him, who was declared
king of the world, sanctify them, they can but hope
(Cf. Rom. 8). Christ stands before God on our behalf. If we enter into judgment, he again shall
speak on our behalf. Let us not say: "Here is something fine for us Christians. But as for the others,
they must be frightened of the judgment." No, because we, ministers, will always be the first unbe-
lievers. On the contrary, let us proclaim this great
truth which, from Christmas on to the Return, is
nothing but: "I bring you good news of a great
joy." Indeed, there is some horror of the judgment:

but it is always God who in Jesus Christ bears it along with sin and death, and it is always we who are invited to let him bear it, in our place, and to live in and upon this faith.

THIRD ARTICLE: THE HOLY SPIRIT AND THE CHURCH

Questions 88-110

PRELIMINARY REMARKS

REMARK I. *On Calvin's Division of the Creed.* Calvin divides the Creed into four parts (Cf. Questions 17-18). He classes in a fourth part faith in the Church, in the communion of saints, in the resurrection of the flesh, and in the life everlasting. Thus, faith in the Holy Spirit constitutes an independent third part. Such a division is not peculiar to Calvin. It is known to several medieval theologians. It must be remarked that although it contributes to point out the importance of the Holy Spirit, nevertheless it does not conform to the obviously trinitarian sense of the ancient Creed which classes the fruits of the Holy Spirit in the same part with the Holy Spirit. On the other hand, Calvin himself interprets his fourth part as being bound up with the third, and we remain faithful to him if we adopt the trinitarian scheme of the Creed.

REMARK II. *On the Connection of the Third with the First Two Articles.* The third article of the Creed (Calvin's third and fourth parts) is a way of answering the question: To what purpose are all these things said about Christ? What do we mean when we confess: I believe in God the Father, I believe in Jesus Christ, the Son of God, our Lord? What profit do we draw from these truths? We realize now that Calvin has already and unceasingly answered these questions. He never presents the assertions of the first two articles as abstract metaphysical truths. On the contrary, he applies himself to show that everything which is said of Christ refers to men. The same is also found in the Creed itself which, by calling Jesus Christ "our Lord," shows that men are immediately embraced in his existence. Calvin stresses this relationship apropos of each Christological truth (Cf. Questions 29, 40-45, 63-64, 71-72, 74-77, 86-87). What we are now about to examine is then not entirely new. It simply is the explicitly evolved consequence of what precedes: "God with us," "God for us."

This article contains four important points:

1. *Faith in the Holy Spirit.* God is the Master, he gives salvation to men whom he bids enter his service.
2. *Faith in the Church.* God creates a place, a means for assuring man's salvation and the service he is called into.

3. *Forgiveness of sins.* This is the gift of salvation under its present aspect.
4. *Resurrection of the flesh and everlasting life.* This is the gift of salvation under its future and everlasting aspect.

What do all these assertions starting with the confession of the Holy Spirit deal with? The general answer, probably, must be: they deal with the needs, aspirations, e.g., the ideals of man reaching for God. Is this answer correct? So it seems at first sight: Yes, they deal with man. We have come to the moment when man receives the Holy Spirit in fellowship with other believers, and participates in God's forgiveness. Yet such a view of things might well be no more than superficial, especially if it claimed to be, strictly speaking, the explanation. No, these assertions do not deal even with the man that reaches for God, and has some needs, aspirations, ideals, and has the possibility and the will to live before God. But again and always and primarily they deal with God, with his intentions and his work. What we now learn explicitly—and it must have already been learned implicitly in the first two articles—is that the intentions, the work and the will of God are totally directed toward man. Because God and man are one in the person of the Christ, we are invited, called into union with God, even carried into it. Note well that as you speak of the Holy Spirit you speak of God; of God, and not of a power or any other sort of fluid. Thus we *enter into* the Creed. It is thus—and thus only —that the Creed can deal with man. Not on account of something man would have brought to God, but because God himself brings himself to man. You can not speak of man in relation to God, revelation, faith, without understanding that man is the object God is reaching for. You can speak of man only *qua* receiver of this gift of God which is God himself.

Whatever is said in the third article—the Church, forgiveness of sins, resurrection of the flesh, everlasting life—therefore refers to Christ. The Church exists because Christ died, rose again and ascended into heaven, and because he shall come again. She is the human, the temporal, the earthly fact corresponding to the Christological reality of his death, of his resurrection, of his ascension, of his reign and return. Forgiveness of sins exists because Christ suffered, died and was buried. The resurrection of the dead is a real hope (and not a pious illusion) on account of Christ's resurrection. Those among you who attended the assembly of the ministerial society at Liestal, will remember the conference of Professor Werner of Berne. It resulted in the complete denial of Christ's resurrection and, consequently, of ours. Here also, there is necessary relationship between the second and the third articles. Finally, everlasting life, the existence following upon resurrection, the new heavens and the new earth, all this would be mere words if right now Jesus Christ were not with that glory. He is its bearer, and we, as members of his body, could not participate in it except through union with him. In conformity with the Creed and the Scripture itself, the Word of God must then be understood as a totality, without separation among various elements.

In sum, the Holy Spirit is nothing other than the relationship between Christ and us. Wherever this relationship is actualized and becomes a fact in men's lives, he is present and acting. This reality of the Holy Spirit is the simplest thing on earth, while it remains of course the greatest mystery.

I. THE HOLY SPIRIT

Questions 88-91

QUESTIONS 88-91.   Let us come to the third part.—
It concerns faith in the Holy Spirit.
What does he do for us?—The intention is that we should know that God, as he has redeemed and saved us by his Son, makes us by his Spirit heirs of this redemption and salvation.
How?—As we have purification in the blood of Christ, so our consciences must be sprinkled by it to be washed (I Pet. 1:19; I John 1:7).
This needs a rather clearer explanation.—I mean that the Spirit of God, while he dwells in our hearts, operates so that we feel the virtue of Christ (Rom. 5:5). For when we conceive the benefits of Christ with the mind, this happens by the illumination of the Holy Spirit; it is by his persuasion that they are sealed in our hearts. In short, he alone gives them a place in us (Eph. 1:13). He regenerates us, and makes of us new creatures (Tit. 3:5). Hence whatever gifts are offered us in Christ, we receive them by virtue of the Spirit.

God's mercies dwell first in God, and not in our hearts. They reside first on Calvary, in Joseph of Arimathea's garden, and not in our consciences. But they change place: they pass from God into us. Here is the new creature, here is the revelation of man. It consists in this event: man receives what he is offered in Jesus Christ. In a way this is quite a simple thing: here you are, one offers you something. Naturally, it does not help you at all if the gift remains in the hand that offers it to you. But if you will take it in your hand, the offer made to you becomes really yours. The word "spirit," in Greek *pneuma,* means: breath, wind, spirit. Wind is a movement of air from one place to another. It was here, and now is there. This is both the image and the reality of man's regeneration by the Holy Spirit: God's Spirit was with God and now is with man. The Holy Spirit is then God going from one place to another, from his place to our place, from the height of his majesty to the baseness of our sin, from the holiness of his glory to the misery of our weakness. The Holy Spirit is God giving us the freedom we were seeking in vain within ourselves: freedom for him.

In the *Institutes,* Calvin describes as follows man's regeneration by the Holy Spirit, this transplantation of God into man: ". . . as long as there is separation between Christ and us, all that he suffered and performed for the salvation of mankind is useless and unavailing to us. To communicate to us what he received from his Father, he must, therefore, become ours, and dwell within us." That is "the secret activity of the Spirit, by which we are introduced to the enjoyment of Christ and all his benefits." (Inst. III. i. 1.)

We see that Calvin, in conformity with the Scripture, does not conceive of the Holy Spirit independently of Jesus Christ. The Holy Spirit is the Spirit of Jesus Christ. Jesus Christ is this movement from God to man. He is the man par excellence, the man naturally united with God, the natural and legitimate son of God. And the rest of us, sinful men, who have not deserved this gift and have no faculty to acquire it, we receive it "in Jesus Christ." It is given us that we may become adoptive sons of God, and brothers of Jesus Christ. The right and the basis for this adoption lie in the fact that Christ is the legitimate and natural son. In Jesus Christ, the Holy Spirit gives us the faculty to exist before God, a faculty that we do not have of ourselves. Who could live before God? the Old Testament asks. No, no man can live before God. But God gives us in Jesus Christ the ability to live before him as the men we are. To live, man needs this act of God. Man in himself would be neither capable of accepting this gift of God nor disposed to accept it. Man in himself would be incompetent over against Christ. Never will we sufficiently emphasize this incompetence. We are too far from Jesus Christ to try to fraternize with him. Were there not the movement of God toward us in Jesus Christ, through the Holy Spirit, our qualification as Christians would be a ridiculous and immensely exaggerated pretension.

What I have just said about man's incompetence is not an anthropological judgment drawn from the knowledge of man in himself, it is not a pessimistic conclusion imposed by the examination of the human situation taken in itself. It is the quite simple consequence of the knowledge that God has given himself to us, it is also the expression of our acknowledgment of this. He who has known the gift of God cannot do otherwise than say: "God has found me, although I have been incapable of finding him. He has loved me, although I have been a rebel. By granting me the resurrection from the dead, he has shown me that I was dead." Such a confession is a criterion of the truth, of the presence of the Holy Spirit.

What here occurs between God and man is no less great a miracle than that of Christmas or of Easter. With the confessing of Christ's birth, the Holy Spirit also is mentioned, and it is not in vain: "Conceived of the Holy Ghost." The same Holy Spirit repeats this miracle of the virgin birth whenever someone comes to believe, to see the whole of his life "in Jesus Christ," to enter the Church, to receive remission of his sins and hope of the everlasting future.

Surely there is a human freedom, the possibility of experiencing and performing certain acts of human knowledge. If all this were not possible, we would not find ourselves at war, and could not even speak now as we do. We would have no feelings, we would have no thought, and we would not even theologize . . . That's why we must not cross out the human element in man. Although we shall see that this element does not explain anything and could not ground our communion with God. For example, think of the story of that paralyzed man (John 5:1-9) who went to the pool of Bethesda, whose waters would only heal the first one to step down into it after the angel had troubled them. They could step down any time they wanted, but it was not always the right moment. God's actual intervention was needed. The connections between human freedom and God's action might thus be represented. Man acts whenever he wants, but his action has import only if it coincides with God's action. Indeed, in the very action of God, it still is a question of man, and of his freedom, and of his life, but of man with God. If we want to understand what God and man are together, we must always raise up our eyes towards heaven, seek what is above, look to the person of Christ. The Holy Spirit, the Spirit of Christ, is, so to speak, the Christ heard, accepted, obeyed by us. The Holy Spirit is not something new beside Christ, or beyond him and, natural or supernatural, in a realm different from his kingdom and his word. Chapters 14-16 of the Gospel according to Saint John put it clearly: "he will take what is mine and declare it to you" (John 16:14). The Holy Spirit is not an increase of what we were given in Christ, but he is the gift itself, actual and living.

Here we are perhaps confronted with the most important mistake, and possibly the only one that is made in every age, with respect to the Holy Spirit. Time and again there are those who always fall into the error of inevitably considering the Holy Spirit as something new and peculiar beside the sole truth of faith and the life of faith. On the one hand, there are people who think they ought to add man's reason to the truth of Christ. They think there is some of the Spirit in man, and believe they ought to and can enhance the truth of Christ by adding to it what we know or think we know by ourselves. And so they proceed to a little blending of Holy Spirit with our varied reasonable spiritualities. On the other hand are those who believe that the Holy Spirit is rather something unreasonable, a sort of mysticism, of transcendental life with astonishing possibilities in contrast to what meets the eye in the person of Christ. Actually they are telling themselves: Poor Jesus, he did not have all these nice things the Holy Spirit has given us. Roman Catholicism, in its very existence, has made this double error concerning the Holy Spirit. It has wanted to add to the person of Christ. And it has done so by way of nature and reason, on the one hand, and by way of mysticism, on the other. On one side: that nice reasonable science, first storey of the knowledge of God, which is natural theology; on the other: saints and miracles, the vast ecstasies of the religious soul and all that glorious life they boast about in the Roman Church. Those who think this is interesting and necessary, why, then, let them have their experience. But, throughout the ages, the Church of Christ has looked for another way, and the church of the Roman confession itself periodically feels the necessity of coming back to this straight but sure way. And not only Roman Catholicism, Protestant modernism, too, fancies that Christ is not enough and tries to complete him with all sorts of religious, humanitarian, scientific experiences presented under the vocable of the Spirit.

But the Holy Spirit distinguishes himself from any other spirit by his absolute identity with the person and the work of Christ. It seems to me that this criterion, which is that of the New Testament, is clear enough. Indeed, the Holy Spirit's revelations are ever new, but of the novelty of Christ, none other. All that is Spirit proceeds from Jesus and results in him.

The gift of the Holy Spirit may be defined as the gift of acknowledging the grace of God in Jesus Christ, and human life under the regime of the Spirit as human existence envisaged "in Jesus Christ." For in Jesus Christ, it is the grace of God that encounters us. Wherever this grace is disregarded, wherever anyone pretends to complete it, wherever life under the regime of the Spirit is no longer this simple and pure acknowledgment, I think we are no longer dealing with the Holy Spirit either. For then, indeed, however religious, however theological or pious, man without Christ is the main concern, but not man in Jesus Christ. The Holy Spirit is spirit of grace, of the forgiveness of sins: hence a spirit of humility wherein the man, his interests and his needs are no longer at the center.

Therefore the Holy Spirit is the criterion of all "spirits." And also he makes judgment of them. Accordingly, the task of the Church of Christ is to discriminate between spirits, thanks to the criterion given to the Church: the Spirit of Christ, the Son of God. As you know, not everybody understood this even in the early Church, especially when the Holy Spirit was thought to be a kind of creature altogether different from God himself, and his substantial divinity was denied.

According to the New Testament, the Holy Spirit is one of the objects of faith. The Creed too declares in conformity with the New Testament: I believe in the Holy Ghost. The Holy Spirit, object of faith, is also an object of prayer: we must not only pray that we may receive the Holy Spirit. We must pray to him. "Veni creator spiritus." A Christian's prayer will always be directed to the Holy Spirit also.

The Holy Spirit brings about the new creation. Being God, his contact with us means a complete change. Where the Holy Spirit is, there we cannot remain as we are. The Holy Spirit attacks us, even

kills us that we may live again. And this must be a
continuous death because the "old" man within us
is a fool who ever again allows himself to come up
to the surface and who ever again needs to be put
back under the surface of the water of baptism, in
order to be drowned. Our new birth is not a fact
accomplished once for all. I think the greatest saint
still needs a complete new birth. For our life in
time is not the life everlasting.

Two more remarks. If we wanted to give a material description of the Holy Spirit, we must say he
is the Spirit of love. And we might also step into
the theology of the Trinity and show that the Holy
Spirit is, already in God himself, the bond between
the Father and the Son, at the same time the means
and the expression of their love. Let us confine ourselves to stressing that the Holy Spirit, being God
"for us," is the very reality of the divine love. The
Holy Spirit is the background of the eternal decree
of God's love, he is the reality of the Covenant
into which God entered before all ages, and which
has been accomplished in Jesus Christ. It is not in
vain that the two definitions of God in the New
Testament are: *God is Spirit* (John 4:24) and *God
is Love* (I John 4:8). And these two are each
other's reality: Spirit of God is his love as manifested, and Love of God is his Spirit as manifesting
Jesus Christ.

Finally let us note that there is a dominion of
the Holy Spirit. It corresponds to the dominion of
Christ, between his resurrection and return.
Christ's resurrection, in a sense, might have been
the end. Does it not declare the end of this world
and the beginning of the Kingdom of God? But
God did not will it so. He inserted between the

resurrection and the Kingdom of God the Dominion of Christ, the dominion of the Holy Spirit.
We may still repent, we may still live on, at once
facing toward resurrection and return, during
these final times which make God's mercy and his
patience manifest to us.•

• In the course of the discussion following upon
Professor Barth's exposition of the Holy Spirit, several
auditors put questions relative to the visibility of the
fruits of the Spirit: is it possible, from the outward
behavior of a Christian, to tell whether or not he
has received the Holy Spirit? Is it possible, after
preaching redemption, to state sanctification precisely
and to say: the work of the Holy Spirit is manifested
in such and such a way? In particular, what should
one think of the gift of healing, of speaking in
tongues, of laying on of hands, and of the baptism of
the Holy Spirit as differing from the baptism of water?

The essentials of Professor Barth's answers may be
summarized as follows:

1. It is certain that the Holy Spirit engenders visible
fruits in believers. But visible unto faith. Only faith
recognizes faith. The signs of the Holy Spirit are indeed real, but theirs is a reality accessible to those
alone who have faith.

2. However, these signs could not constitute absolute criteria, as though we would have God's last
judgment on this earth and in our hands. God remains above all Christian life and does not surrender
into our hands so that we might no longer have to
fear his judgment and hope in his mercy.

3. As regards special manifestations—speaking in
tongues, healing of sicknesses, etc.—they are possible
consequences of the gift of the Holy Spirit. They
could not be conditions which alone authorize those
who meet them to declare that they possess the Holy

II. THE CHURCH

Questions 92-100

QUESTIONS 92-100. Let us proceed.—The fourth part follows, in which we confess our belief in one Holy Catholic Church.

What is the Church?—The body and society of believers whom God has predestined to eternal life.

Is this article also necessary to belief?—Yes, in-

———————

Spirit. Paul (I Cor. 12-14) speaks of such gifts in a restrictive way. Let us gather around the substance of the Gospel, around the Cross and the Resurrection! Here is our bread. And so long as we need bread we may not call out for cake! Once we have been fed with bread, then, for dessert perhaps, we shall receive all these delicacies: speaking in tongues, healing, etc.

4. Finally, when extraordinary things are claimed, should it not be asked whether all the extraordinary mentioned in the New Testament is not quite simply contained and presented to the Church in the sacraments? If we understand the realism of baptism and of the Lord's Supper, we will have all the Christian ordinary and all the extraordinary. Now, what I bump into is the assertion that in addition to the Word of God—which may be proclaimed, heard, obeyed, and which is something clear for everybody, for children and for adults—there may be for an elect audience, for special Christians, particular gifts pretended to be indispensable to some state of perfection. If all those who advocate these special manifestations want to be heard in the Church, let them show these to her and, then, I hope that the whole Church will be capable of obeying the voice of truth! [Editor]

deed: if we would not render Christ's death ineffective and reduce to nothing all that has hitherto been said. For the one effect of all this is that there be a Church.

You think, then, that up to now the cause of salvation has been treated and its foundation shown, when we explained that by Christ's merits and intercession we were received into the love of God, and this grace as confirmed in us by the virtue of the Holy Spirit. But now the effect of all this is to be explained, that by the very facts our faith may stand the firmer.—It is so.

In what sense then do you call the Church holy? —In this sense, that all whom God chooses he justifies, and remakes in holiness and innocence of life (Rom. 8:29), so that in them his glory may be displayed. This is what Paul intends, when he affirms that Christ sanctifies the Church which he redeemed, that it might be glorious and free from all stain (Eph. 5:25).

What is the meaning of the attribute catholic or universal?—By it we are taught that, as there is one head of all the faithful, so all ought to unite in one body, so that there may be one Church spread throughout the whole earth, and not a number of Churches (Eph. 4:3; I Cor. 12:12, 27).

But what is the force of adding forthwith the Communion of Saints?—This is put here to express more clearly that unity which exists between the members of the Church. At the same time it is indicated that whatever benefits God bestows upon the Church serve the common good of all, since all have communion with each other.

But is this holiness which you attribute to the Church now perfect?—Not yet: that is, so long as it battles in this world. For it always labors under infirmities, nor is it ever wholly purged of the vestiges of vice, until it completely adheres to Christ its Head by whom it is sanctified. But is it possible to know this Church other than by the faith with which it is believed?— There is indeed also a visible Church of God, which he has described to us by sure marks and signs. But strictly this question concerns the company of those who, by secret election, he has adopted for salvation; and this is not always visible with the eyes nor discernible by signs.

Calvin starts here a new section: the Church. All that follows: forgiveness of sins, resurrection of the dead, the life everlasting, is hence contained, for Calvin, in the article on the Church. In Questions 104-105 we see why Calvin has these articles follow upon that of the Church: "Because no one obtains it, unless he has previously been united with the people of God" and "Those who disrupt from the Body of Christ and split its unity into schisms are quite excluded from the hope of salvation, so long as they remain in dissidence of this kind."

On the other hand, in Question 94, Calvin declares that the Church is the fruit of Christ's death. And, since we participate in Christ's death through the Holy Spirit, the doctrine of the Holy Spirit results, according to Calvin, in that of the Church.

Thus the benefits of the Holy Spirit are conferred upon believers by means of the Church, mother of the faithful. In the Creed, the same holds: the Church precedes the individual and particular gifts. The modernist conception of the Church is exactly the reverse: first of all they speak of what the individual receives, then of the free incorporation into a "church" of these lucky individuals who have individually received their salvation.

But with Calvin, and as well in the Creed as in the New Testament, the body of Christ exists prior to its members: There is first the College of the Twelve Apostles, then the individual believers.

ECCLESIA

The Hebrew קהל, the Greek ἐκκλησία, transcribed into the Latin *ecclesia,* mean assembled "convocation"; Calvin calls it: a company. Imagine citizens called by the trumpet and rushing from everywhere. They are present, they form a company, the company of the faithful, of those who, called by God's faithfulness, have responded with their faithfulness. It is God who has convoked them. It is important to note that the Church is not formed by a human gathering of people who would have the same opinions, but by a divine convocation that constitutes into a corps individuals until then scattered at the mercy of their opinions. The nineteenth century was certainly in error, when it understood the Church as a "religious society," a term taken over by jurisprudence and which, it is to be hoped, will disappear from twentieth-century official documents.

"The body and society of believers whom God has predestined to eternal life," says Calvin. Here I allow myself a small criticism of Calvin. As a matter of fact, it is surprising that Calvin should follow after his own idea and speak only of eternal life, that is, the individual goal of believers gathered into the Church. It seems to me that if we want to keep the order of the New Testament we must say: God has ordained and chosen them into his temporal and eternal service, and, consequently, into everlasting life. The notion of service should not be missing. In the New Testament, they did not come to the Church merely so that they might be saved and happy, but that they might have the signal privilege of serving the Lord. And we should bring to the fore the benefit that we receive from service and work in the Church. Of course this service leads to the life everlasting that is its result and reward. In a sense, it is already the life everlasting. But still this should be said! Still it should become clear that the life everlasting cannot be understood without this service! The "company" that Calvin rightly speaks of now becomes wholly meaningful: we are in the service, in the military service. The Church forms a body distinguished by the call that founded her, by the promise given to those who are the constituents of this body, by the goal they seek after and the service they accomplish in it.

HOLY

Holiness, in the Bible, is the fact of being set apart. The holiness of the Church will purely and simply consist in the fact that the Church has both the benefit of listening to the Word of God and that of hoping. The Church is the place that God wants to bless, where God wants his work to be praised and declared to the world. Holiness means: separation from all that is not the Church. In the world there are other communities than that of the Church: family, school, society, State. None of these communities is identical with the Church, and the Church is limited by none of these distinctions. She pervades them all. A limited church is a sick church. A "bourgeois" church is as sick as a "proletarian" church. Indeed, because of her holiness, the true Church limited neither on one side nor the other. She is free. Indeed, she may have very close connections with these other communities. But she should never confuse herself with any of them.

What is the communion of saints? The term is twofold: the genitive "sanctorum" of the Latin text is both masculine and neuter, and it must be interpreted with its two genders. *a*) Communion among the saints, among men whom God, through his Word, has set apart and constituted into a Church. *b*) Communion in sacred things, communion created by sacred things: the Word, preaching, sacraments, God's work, commission received in the Church.

The term "holy" applied to the Church, to God's work, and to believers has then no direct moral meaning. It does not mean that these people are particularly suited to come near to God, to deserve his revelation, that these things are particularly adapted to represent God. Rather, holiness is conferred upon them as a matter of the fact that God has chosen them, both men and things, in order to reveal himself in them.

CATHOLIC

The notion of catholicity is quite near that of holiness. The Church, being different from any other human community, thereby is catholic, that is, universal. She is limited by no barrier, either of state, or of race, or of culture. Exclusively and properly belonging to no one, the Church belongs to everyone. She is really "national" because she is really "independent." She belongs to every man because she belongs to no man in particular.

THE LIMITS OF THE CHURCH

We have just looked into the constituency of the Church, as described by Calvin; as such, she has limits that should be known so that we may define her task and her living conditions.

1. *The Relationship of the Church with the Kingdom of God.* The Church announces the Kingdom of God, she is not the Kingdom of God. Her *raison d'être* is found only within the extent of this intermediary time when the victory of God has been declared, but has not yet been made manifest in glory. Within the time of God's patience, she announced the grace and judgment accomplished in Jesus Christ, which on his return will be revealed in glory and in public. But in the Kingdom of God there shall

be no Church any longer (Cf. Rev. 21:22). Then, Jeremiah's prophecy shall be accomplished (31:34): "And no longer shall each man teach his neighbor and each his brother, saying, 'Know the Lord' for they shall all know me, from the least of them to the greatest, says the Lord."

The body of Christ shall continue to exist, of course, but not under the aspect of the Church. The Church is the temporal aspect of the body of Christ and its members. As such, she bears every stamp of human imperfection. She lies under the sign of the "Not yet." And there is no reason to be surprised and saddened that this provisional condition shows up, at every age in the time of the Church, in a really humiliating and pitiful manner. On the other hand, let us not fancy, if the situation is looking a little improved, that we are at last stepping into the Kingdom of Heaven. Let us not believe for instance that the Kingdom of Heaven is come because we have a somewhat better theology now than we had fifty years ago. It is a theology that's just a little bit better! After all, undoubtedly, those who will come after us, and even the youngest among us, will witness and perhaps make new changes, there will be new dangers and, who knows? a new liberalism may be seen reappearing . . . In man's history all things recur again, until the end of this history. It goes on turning around as on that stained-glass window of Basel on which there is a little man on top of a wheel, who goes around clear down to the bottom and then goes on up to the opposite rim of the wheel. This is not just an illustration of human life, but quite as well of Christian life and the life of the Church between resurrection and return. This must be reckoned with. The Church is a provisional aspect of the Kingdom of God. The Kingdom of God is quite near; this is noticeable. Without that, there would be no movements, no awakenings, no reformations. He stands at the door, he knocks, while we are within and wait. He is quite near to us. But the door stands between him and us, the glorious door through which the King of Glory will make his entrance. Let us keep from forgetting this door—which has not been stepped through as yet—and from indulging in spiritual pride, Christian and theological and ecclesiastical. They would really have to be pitied, these young friends of mine, if they would cultivate a sort of "pontificalism" because they know something of the Word of God. They think they know now more and better than their fathers knew. Let them beware of the deceptions that may follow upon such a presumption! Human life is short and yet, I assure you, long enough. After the first discoveries made in theology come along those years which do not "fly" as it says in the song. Very often they drag along. And the year has fifty-two weeks with as many sermons, as many catechisms, as many visits, to be busy with. One can become tired and a little bored. Please, no unseasonable enthusiasm, my young friends. We live under the sign of the "Not yet." As Calvin said, God holds us by the bridle like a walking horse. This horse can walk, but if it reared up it would run into trouble or overstrain itself. Walk slowly, knowing that it shall not be you who will snatch the Kingdom of God and who will bring it down on earth. You shall declare it, that is all. And this will be your foundation, a sure, a peaceful, a joyful foundation.

The Church is, therefore, not the only aspect of the present Dominion of Christ, and of the Kingdom of God foretold and to come. The New Testament teaches us that there are no powers in the world of which Jesus Christ is not the King and Master, and which are not bound to serve his designs, even against their will. The Church is then not only limited by the Kingdom of God to come, but by the present Dominion of Christ. We must not be surprised if it is true that God, in every time, also has other servants than us Christians, than us ministers. Christians and ministers oftentimes behave as though they alone were servants of God! Well, they certainly are never the only ones! The Old Testament tells us that the heavens declare the glory of God. This glory of God is continually being declared in the course of history, in nature, in the world, without our hearing it, without our understanding it. Perhaps, from time to time, we may fancy we understand some of it. But it is none of our business. Yet it is real. God has not shirked the world. God has not forsaken the world. He is present in the present Dominion of Christ.

2. *The Church, the State, and the "Angels."* The State is one of these manifestations of the power and the love of God beside the Church. It is a real ordinance of God, a divine institution according to Romans 13. It is a power in the service of God—as well as the Church. The State also participates in the weakness, in the human-

ity, and in the evilness of men. But if it is looked
at side by side with the Church, perhaps one
would be disposed to forgive it some of its faults
. . . The Church is not all. That too is a comfort. God's power of justice and love is wielded
outside of ecclesiastical weakness and unworthiness.

In general, we cannot assert: the hand of God
is *here* in the world. However, there is a difference between the man who walks with the assurance that God reigns and the man who does
not know it. God reigns not only in this ministerial house but also in this more worldly street;
not only in the Church but also among all these
people who are picking grapes and will drink on
Sunday and will dance. God is also among our
soldiers, among our national councillors and
among all this nation. They are all certainly in
the hands of God and God is ever the same.
These people are different, and we too are different. But one thing is sure: whatever happens in
the world, it is God who reigns in Jesus Christ.
Often one believes it. Often also one is at pain
to believe it. The essential thing is that this is
true.

It is important that we take the Church seriously. But we must not take ourselves too
seriously as ministers. Do not fancy that in your
parish you are God's angel with the flaming
sword! You are just a simple minister permitted
to preach the good news. Be sure that there are
other "angels" (that is, messengers) than you!
They may be very odd angels, but they are angels! Tell yourself: I will do my best but at the
same time I know that the coming of the King-

dom does not depend on me. It is not I who ought to accomplish everything. All is accomplished. My manse is not a little island of peace and justice in a sea of injustice . . .

3. *The Task of the Church.* What we have just looked into must not lead us into error regarding the dignity of the Church. The Church is not the sole place of Christ's Dominion. Still, she is quite special a place: the place where God in Jesus Christ is not only present, but declared as being present, confessed as being present. She is the place where all pray and where all are together in the communion of the remembrance of the Lord and the hope of his return, where all commune at the Lord's table, where together with others all eat his body, and where together all drink his blood. The Church and the world under the Dominion of Christ must not be confused. The Church is the body of Christ in the world. She spreads his light, she declares his grace, she proclaims his judgment. Having received the light, she is the light of the world. Our considerations in the first two points do not authorize a relaxation of the zeal for the Church. We in the Church, we know, we have heard God's call and we are commissioned to convey it on to the world; for the world is its concern. We have to tell the world, on behalf of God, that the grace of God is given to it, that the time is short and the time it is still given is on account of God's patience in view of repentance. Natural man always believes his time to be infinite, that all time is at his disposal. The Christian knows and declares that this time is short, that in real-

ity it is already up, that the dice are cast and that there is time left solely to recognize the fact. The only advantage of the Church over against the world is that the Church knows the real situation of the world. Christians know what non-Christians do not. Nevertheless, it will not be too surprising to meet often enough people outside the Church who know all this almost a little better than Christians with all their Christianity. It happens that a simple person is met who is not a churchgoer, who does not read the Bible, but who lives in the manner one should live, in this acceptant and peaceful manner in which the Dominion of Christ is noticeable. Only, he does not know it, he does not witness to it consciously and intelligibly. It belongs to the Church to witness to the Dominion of Christ clearly, explicitly, and consciously.

THE LIVING CONDITIONS OF THE CHURCH

In point of fact, we have just looked into the meaning of the Church and we can now point out her living conditions.

1. *The Government of the Church.* The government of the Church needs to conform with the foundation of the Church. The Church was not founded by men, by a few persons who, being on the right side of the fence, were gathered together to cultivate their spiritual needs. The Church was founded by the Christ who called his disciples. The initiative was not taken by the

apostles, but by their master who created for them the commission of the apostolate and entrusted them with it. Nor is the government of the Church, consequently, the business of a human initiative. It is an act of obedience unto the Lord of the Church. The Lord of the Church is Jesus Christ alone, such as he exists in time, that is, in the Scripture. Thus, no government, either monarchical or aristocratic or democratic, of the Church shall be able, as such, to pretend to authority. Rather, it shall possess authority only to the extent in which it serves Jesus Christ, that is to say, concretely, in which it submits all its decisions to the criterion of the Scripture. We shall not then have any fundamental reason to prefer the aristocratic to the democratic system, or conversely. For in the Church we are not dealing with either "someone" or "some ones" or "everyone," but with the One: the Lord. The essential of Church government is not its outward form, but its submission to the Scripture.

2. *The Specific Work of the Church.* From what we saw of the limitations of the Church, the work of the Church should be understood in an equally—and salutarily—limited manner. Many tasks are needed in the world: the building of a better society, of a better economy, of a more perfected monetary system. It is quite natural that men would like to live in a better organized society than this one whose remains we see around at present. It is quite understandable that the whole world today appeals to the future, and that they seek to lay out charts for the Ocean. However, it is out of the Church's line to seek to

improve human society and to make plans and projects for this purpose. The work of the Church is more modest: to call men, to recall to them that God reigns and is present, clearly to tell that man does not live by his own strength, but by the grace of God. It belongs to other human undertakings—equally submitted to God even though they yet ignore it—to build a better society.

As much might be said of the Church. The Church is not the State and she does not have to replace it. Indeed the Church, guardian of the veritable interest of the world, has a very special, a very concrete interest in the existence of the State. She knows the State as a divine institution and she teaches submission to the State. She proclaims the holiness of this divine institution and should protest against its violation. However, she should not go into such and such politics, she should not try to bind the Gospel to some political party. She shall be able to give advice, to protest and pass resolutions. But, as Church, she should not give her allegiance to any particular politics.

The same holds for the intellectual realm. The work of the Church should not consist in publishing the true philosophy. Indeed, this too is a task to be accomplished, but not by the Church. The Church, here too, must restrict herself to her proper work: the proclamation of the Gospel, the exegesis of the Bible and of the Confession of Faith. Constantly, the Church runs the danger of unduly extending her task. How many ministers busy themselves with a multiplicity of things, and take the risk of forsaking the sole thing necessary to the Church! One always ought to ask oneself: Do I have any business in that, I, a minister, I, a preacher, I, a Christian? Do not misunderstand me: this is not evasion. This is a concentration of the Work. We must come back to our sheep. Not all sheep are ours. Let us first attend to ours. Let us trust that the task of the Church is necessary enough that we should dedicate ourselves to it entirely, and that theology is sufficiently important that we shall not also be interested in philosophy. By thus concentrating her work, the Church will render a service to every laborer. She will fill her specific role, and that is God's demand.

3. *The Humility of the Church.* (Cf. Questions 99-100.) The Creed requests that we "believe" the Church. This is because the Church is an object of faith and not of sight. Let us clearly make this distinction: it is not a question of believing in an invisible Church, but—seeing the visible Church—of believing in the invisible Church through her earthly and present expression. Let us not sever the present humility from the glory to come! It is in the humility of the flesh that Christ appeared, and what is true of the head is true also of the body.

4. *The Faithfulness to the Visible Church.* There are so many visible churches: Roman, Eastern, Lutheran, Reformed, National, Independent, etc. And there are the smaller communities, and the sects. How can this be helped? Often, faith in the Church Universal is understood as the

faith in a kind of summary of what is best in each denomination. So, one hovers over every church and belongs to none. According to the New Testament, to believe the Church is first to belong to one's church, whatever it may be, and within it to confess the Church Universal. From then on, one will be able to see what is good in other churches, is more faithful to the Word of God and will learn from it, and maybe will transfer from one to another church. But the important thing is never to separate the visible Church from the invisible Church. Let us not hover over the clouds: to believe is to live. To live is to labor. To labor is to be here and not there. Concretely to believe the Church is to accept concretely to live within a church.

5. *The Two Aspects of the Church.* The Church, such as Calvin defines her in keeping with the Creed and the Scripture, hence has a twofold aspect: she is humble because she is still earthly and subjected to human weakness. She is glorious because she announces the glorious kingdom of God. She is a very dark mirror in which we perceive a very bright light. We ought to keep from two dangers: one consists in despising the Church (as people did readily enough twenty years ago), by comparing her with the kingdom of God and getting rid of her under the pretext that she is not the kingdom; if we do so, we betray the very kingdom which wants to be announced through the weakness of the Church; one becomes incapable of really laboring for this kingdom. The other danger consists in exalt-

ing the Church, in forgetting that she is not the kingdom, that she lives under the sign of the "Not yet" we spoke about.

The consequence for us of the real situation of the Church within this "short" time, between the Resurrection and the Return, is what I should like to call a hope brought under discipline. Discipline for the Church and hope for the kingdom of God. But these two ought to be conjoined always. It is given us to hope for the kingdom of God, but given also is the order not to anticipate the times, rather to know how to live, with humility, in the present lowness of the Church, although she is bearer of the glorious message.

III. THE FORGIVENESS OF SINS

Questions 101-105

Introductory Remark on the Last Three Assertions of the Creed. The Holy Spirit being the dominator and the donor, the Church being the place and the means of God's glory and the human salvation until Christ's return, the last three assertions—forgiveness of sins, resurrection of the flesh, life everlasting—describe the work of God in mankind. By reason of its origin, this work is founded in Christ. But it is now important to consider its effects, indeed without severing it from Christ who is its origin, but also without fancying that it may be unnecessary (having contemplated Christ) still to contemplate Christ's gifts to the Church. These last three assertions hence deal with human life considered in the light of Jesus Christ's death, resurrection and exaltation.

Forgiveness of sins: consideration of human life in the light of the death of Jesus Christ. The present time, characterized by the fact that Jesus Christ died within time, in its entirety bears the stamp of this death. By the fact that Christ died within time, this time is no longer infinite: it is finite, its end is nearing, and in fact it has even already come to an end. Within this time also, sins are forgiven. The time of our lives, of our era, the time of the Church have as their specific characteristic that sins are forgiven.

Resurrection of the flesh: consideration of human life in the light of the resurrection of Christ. Here is the passage from the present time into the time to come. Corresponding to the resurrection of Christ, our Head, we believe in the resurrection of the flesh, which is the passage of man, of mankind, of the world, from the present time into the time to come, from this world into a new world.

Life everlasting: consideration of human life in the light of the exaltation of Christ, of his reign on the right hand of God. Here we are beyond the passage, within the new time ushered in by the resurrection.

It is important to understand the forgiveness of sins, the resurrection of the flesh and the life everlasting not as metaphysically independent, as historical or metahistorical, truths or realities, but as the aspect of human life in its relation to the history of Jesus Christ. One cannot speak of forgiveness of sins, of resurrection of the flesh, and of life everlasting independently of Christ. Their truth and their reality are exclusively within the person of Christ. But this person shines forth. We may step into the light that shines from him and live there. At this point our thinking must be done with much consistency: everything we are about to take up is primarily true of the Christ alone. Yet it is given us to walk in the steps of Christ, and this must be understood with the least reservation possible: we are following a chief, we are walking after a leader.

QUESTIONS 101-105. What comes next?—I believe in the forgiveness of sins.

What do you mean by the word forgiveness?— I mean that God by his gratuitous goodness forgives and pardons the faithful their sins, so that they are not summoned to judgment nor is punishment exacted from them.

It follows then that in no sense do we by our own satisfaction merit the pardon of sins which we obtain from God?—That is true. For Christ alone, by paying the penalty, made satisfaction. As for us, no compensation from our side procures what we have from God: we receive this benefit gratuitously out of his sheer liberality.

Why do you subjoin the forgiveness of sins to the Church?—Because no one obtains it, unless he has previously been united with the people of God, cultivates this unity with the body of Christ up to the end, and thus testifies that he is a true member of the Church.

You conclude from this that outside the Church there is no salvation but only damnation and ruin?—Certainly. Those who disrupt from the body of Christ and split its unity into schisms are quite excluded from the hope of salvation, so long as they remain in dissidence of this kind.

Generally speaking, the forgiveness of sins describes the present living condition of man. But this present life, under the sign of the remission of sins, is in fact the guaranty of life everlasting: because there is forgiveness of sins death—the wages of sin—is overcome and life is promised.

Let us notice that human life, under the sign of the Cross of Jesus Christ, is twice illuminated: 1. It is qualified as sinful, as condemned. The Holy Spirit communicates to us the revelation of the condemnation we do deserve. We have to live in the knowledge of this divine wrath and under the crushing weight of this condemnation. 2. But this is only a part of the truth of forgiveness of sins, and the smallest: at the same time the Holy Spirit communicates to us the revelation of our acquittal.

Question 102: Remission and acquittal mean to cross out. God states that our sin exists. But he crosses it out. According to Calvin, sins do come under judgment to be punished, but they are not punished in our own person. There is a punishment, and a necessary punishment, but we are not those it strikes.

Question 103: There is no room for human merit in this affair. We are not the cause of forgiveness, of liberation from sin and of the liberty that follows. On the other hand, we cannot reward God for that. Indeed, there is a necessary thanksgiving, but this thanksgiving will always be insufficient,

it will never be equal to what God has given us.
Thus God is the great liberal. For the Bible and for
Calvin, there is no other liberalism than this liberalism of God who does not want to tally up his accounts with man.

Questions 104-105. To explain the somewhat
energetic thesis of Calvin "Without the Church no
salvation," we had better keep in mind the order
of succession: Christ, Spirit, Church. It is not at all
because we belong in the Church that we benefit
by Christ. It is because we have received the benefits of Christ that we belong in the Church, and
that we necessarily belong in her. The manhood of
Christ becomes ours now. To live in possession of
the Holy Spirit, to live as members of the Church
means: to undergo the efficacy of Christ's manhood.
Think of John 6. A believer, he who lives in the
fellowship of Christ, eats his body and drinks his
blood. The Lord's Supper is the sign of this real
and direct union. Jesus lived for us. Our lives can
only be the realization of this "for you" of the Gospel. How could possibly one know Christ without
accepting to be a member of his body?

Anyone who receives the Holy Spirit and becomes a member of the Church becomes Jesus
Christ's property. Being his property, he becomes
the object of his responsibility. By living really
with Christ, man is no longer responsible for himself: Christ is responsible for him. How to meet
God? How to have a good conscience? How to live
worthily? How to live a life worth the trouble of
being lived? How to play a satisfying part in my
environment, in mankind? All these questions are

removed, are crossed out. It does not belong to us to decide what we are and what we are worth. We do not have to answer this question: what to do with our lives? Jesus Christ answered it by entering himself into the act in our place, and by taking on the responsibility for our lives. Fortunately— for without that we would be quite pitiable. What could we show forth on the hour of our death, on the time our human lives have been played out? We should say perhaps: Why, I thought well, I worked well, I prayed well. I did this and that, and I was this or that. But what would that be worth in the face of death and judgment? Nothing or nobody can suffice, except the one who overcame death.

Receiving the Holy Spirit, becoming members of the Church, We receive the advantage of an exchange as Paul calls it (καταλλαγή), II Cor. 5; Rom. 5). Ordinarily this is translated by "reconciliation," but in fact it should read "exchanger." There occurs, through the grace of God in Jesus Christ, an exchange between God and us. In Jesus Christ, God gives us his life and takes ours. Our life becomes his concern and his life becomes our concern. Whether we are sinners is no longer our concern, nor is it any longer our business. It is God's business who, in our place, wills to be the sinner. Therefore we do not have any longer to answer these questions: "What man are you? Do you know that you are a sinner?" Indeed, we know we are. But that is not interesting any longer, because, sinner or not, God put himself in my place, took over what I do and what I shall yet do! He took over all my distress. And now, so to speak, I am outside of myself. And I look to him. And here he is, Jesus

Christ. Look! On his person, all that I am, all that displeases me in myself and in others. All human misery is in him. And all the complaints people might address to me, and all the complaints I might address to others, now run against Jesus Christ. Behold the Lamb of God who takes away the sin of the world. Anyone who wants to attack and accuse me and anyone who wants to accuse my neighbor and accuse the world, well, then, let him accuse him who is charged with the responsibility. God attended to mankind, and he did it seriously. This is the depth of his mercy. He is not content with criticizing us, with lamenting for us and adding that, despite our failings, he loves us. This is fine, but that's precisely how the Rev. Mr. X also acts in relation to his parishioners. God's attitude is more than that: he does what no one can do for others. He steps into their distress, he makes it really totally his. He takes it on, he takes it over, and he takes it away. He is strong enough to do it and he is good enough to will to do so. In the person of his Son, God suffers his own judgment against sin. He is at once judge and judged. And it is thus that sin is blotted out radically, efficaciously.

That we may better understand forgiveness of sins, we have still to consider how grievous sin is. Remission is no weakness of God. God takes us seriously. But he takes himself seriously too, himself, his law, and his will. Sin is not a child's prank that God will tolerate. It is very grievous, and God can blot it out only by entering the lists with the totality of his Godhead. "God with us." This is more than a feeling of God's presence: it is his very presence. God puts himself in our place, like a teacher who sits at the desk of a schoolboy and then tells him: "Until now you've been drawing all by yourself; I want now to make your drawing for you." And he begins to draw for him a nice drawing in his schoolboy's exercise book. And the child is at his side and he is looking on. God tells us similarly: "My friend, here I am in your place. Until now you have been quite happy or quite unhappy to be there, to live, to mind your business, to be responsible. Move away, that I may set myself to this, and you sit at my side." By sitting at the master's side, let us hope that the child will learn something. He is not inactive; he looks on, he follows, he learns.

A passage from Paul sums up what we have just said. Gal. 2:20: "It is no longer I who live, but Christ who lives in me; and the life I now live in the flesh I live by faith in the Son of God, who loved me and gave himself for me." If we understand this verse, we have understood everything. This is the whole of faith and of Christian life.

But you wonder now: is it really the whole? Is there not in the Christian faith yet something other than forgiveness of sins? It should be noticed that the Apostles' Creed, speaking of Christian life in the present time, mentions only the forgiveness of sins. Luther and Calvin did the same, they who essentially put forth one truth alone: the forgiveness of sins, which they used then to call justification by faith. Were they right in thus narrowing down all Christianity, all the Christian life and faith to one single point? I think the answer should be: Yes, the Creed and the Reformers were right.

For the forgiveness of sins is the basis, the sum, the criterion, of all that may be called Christian life or faith.

Now, is Christianity not a new law, a new rule of life as people took to understanding it from the second century on? Many Christian writers, polemicizing against pagans, seem to see no other differences between paganism and Christianity than those pertaining to morals: The early Christians would be those who had a new knowledge of what God demands of man. And they mentioned— as is done today—love, modesty, temperance. I should not want to remove this aspect of Christianity. Yes, the Gospel is also a new law. But it differs from any other law to which we might compare it. And when it does not differ any longer, it becomes again a sort of Jewish legalism, as is the case, for example, with Roman Catholicism, and with all sorts of variants of modern protestantism. In what does the Gospel differ from Jewish and pagan morals, so that we could not compare it to them? The answer should be: precisely in this that all this new law, all this new "commandment" of the Gospel rests on the forgiveness of sins. Christian life is the life at once comforted and troubled, liberated and disciplined, because it is founded on the forgiveness of sins, which takes a man out of himself and introduces into him the principle of divine life. Understand Christian morals as you wish: pull it on the legalistic side, or on the liberal side, understand it as a comfort or as a warning, be mystical or activistic, this matters little after all provided your comfort, your trouble, your liberty, your discipline are founded on the fact of the forgiveness of sins, provided your life is situated on this movement of transfer from God to you and from you to God; provided the exchange between God's life and your life takes place; provided you are the child who looks on the teacher drawing (as in our illustration above); provided we are these displaced men, put out of themselves—and in reality having found in God their own lives—who are no longer responsible, who are no longer their own masters and who know that someone else manages their business. Once again, there are many Christian possibilities, and we should not look for quarrels on this subject: Gentlemen, put down your stakes! Yes, gentlemen, put them down. These are stakes to be put down and we are like children who are allowed to play their games with a little more secularism or pietism; no matter, provided the game of their liberty is permitted by the forgiveness of sins, and is founded on it. Let us not relapse any more into false responsibility, into that pride, into that search for self-justification before God and before men. Let us be sure of our Christian life, but let us be sure of it according to the Word: "What is done with the flesh, let it be done with the faith in the Son of God."

It was also said: The Gospel is above all a new and better knowledge of God. You know that in the first century, there was this tendency, called "gnostic," whereby the whole of Christianity was understood as a wisdom, a philosophy, embodying and disclosing the mysteries of God and of the world. Does not Calvin himself say, at the beginning of his Catechism, that the chief end of man is to know God? Here too there were abuses: Christianity often became a philosophy, a dogmatics, and this is unquestionably a danger. It is always a danger and a seduction to write such thick volumes of dogmatics! I am not so sure that this knowledge of God we take the permission to spread out is the Gospel! But then, here too, there is a permitted, a legitimate knowledge. To know God means to know Jesus Christ as the Son of God, to understand the Son as the son of the Father, and the Father as the father of the Son. To understand the work of the Godhead as the creating and redeeming work of God. And whoever has understood that the ground of this knowledge is the forgiveness of sins, he shall have the right, on this basis, to think and be a "liberal" or an "orthodox." Each will have to play his game: a serious and very difficult game. Let this child now play his game, and do not disturb him, please! Let us be clement, nice, towards these poor intellectualists! Christian life does also consist in the knowledge of God. Intelligence is not a bad thing. This "gnosis" of which the New Testament speaks sometimes can be very close to faith. And then those who despise intelligence perhaps find that the grapes are too sour . . . But this knowledge should not be severed from the forgiveness of sins. It does not deal with a work intended to glorify man and his thought, but with an act of "acknowledgment" (in the twofold meaning of the word) performed by him who has acknowledged the exchange effected by God between divine and human life.

There are still other conceptions of Christian life; all of them subject like ethics or knowledge to the forgiveness of sins, thus relative to something else than themselves. Such is the case for sacramental communion, stressed in the Catholic wing. When this communion is well oriented, when it depends on the forgiveness of sins, it is a good thing. Let then the Catholics play their game. But we do not need to join in with them when they put the game above forgiveness of sins, when they substitute for forgiveness of sins what may only be its consequence, when they identify the work of the Church with the work of God. Nevertheless, we have to learn from them, too, when they remind us of sacramental life.

We might continue and review every aspect of Christianity: e.g., psychological aspect, sociological aspect. Indeed, Christianity is also a lifting up of the soul and a renewal of society. But each of these to the extent in which it is inspired, borne, created, by the forgiveness of sins.

I should say, therefore, that this answer, given by the Creed and the Reformers to the question: "What is Christian life?" is complete and correct. Everything is included in the forgiveness of sins. And any principle independent of forgiveness of sins can only be un-Christian, insufficient, and in the last resort dangerous both to the Christian life and to human life.

IV. THE RESURRECTION OF THE FLESH *

Questions 106-109

In the resurrection of the flesh (with which Paul dealt so often, especially in I Cor. 15) just as in the

---

*The French text throughout the Catechism reads consistently *"résurrection de la chair"* and not *"des corps."* [Translator]

forgiveness of sins, we are concerned with man's life. But there is a difference between forgiveness of sins and resurrection of the flesh. So to speak, one is the reverse of the other. The forgiveness of sins starts with temporal human existence and places it in its relation to eternity. Inversely, the resurrection of the flesh starts with eternity and ushers human existence into it. Forgiveness of sins opens the perspective of eternity to human existence. Resurrection of the flesh, we might say, opens the perspective of human life to eternity: you will find human life in eternity.

Notice that it is not a question of death, but of resurrection. Indeed, resurrection presupposes death. But, by mentioning only resurrection, the Creed presents death as already overcome, it introduces it into the movement of God's victory. The goal of human life is not death, but resurrection. And in the light of the Gospel, death is no more than a passage.

Resurrection of the *flesh* is spoken of. In the Creed as in the New Testament, the notion of flesh designates the whole man. The resurrection of the flesh is therefore identical neither with immortality of the soul, nor with resurrection of the body alone. It means the resurrection of the whole man, such as he is and not such as he ought to have been, of the real man, miserable and sinful, and not of any ideal man. This real man shall rise again; his future lies beyond death. The end of his life is not death, but resurrection, which is a new beginning, and the life everlasting. Thus resurrection crowns human life and ushers it into a new life. When I say: "to crown human life," please notice right away that this is a very miraculous crown for the earthly life of man as such, the life condemned to death and lost. But, being Christians, we understand human life no longer in itself, but in Jesus Christ risen.

In the light of Jesus Christ's resurrection, human life thus appears to be set apart, sanctified. With forgiveness of sins, our justification was in question. Sanctification is a little different: it means that those who are justified, admitted by God, acknowledged as his children, could not be lost. What is God's cannot be overcome by death. What is God's possesses a pledge of life eternal. This pledge is the faith in the resurrection of the flesh set in our hearts by the Holy Spirit.

Thus the Holy Spirit has not only a psychological but also a physical characteristic. Those who believe in the Word of God receive a real seed of a real new life. The Word of God is often called a seed fallen into the earth and beginning to grow. This is not just a parable. There is a beginning of eternal life within this life. Remember also certain passages of Saint Paul, where the Apostle speaks of the Holy Spirit as a pledge, a guaranty. Together with the Holy Spirit we receive, in time, something that overcomes fatality and the limits of death. We live, we die, and, living unto death, going this way of ours which sooner or later will end up in the grave at the cemetery, living our mortal lives, we bear the beginning of another life.

Human life, insofar as it is Christian life, may hence be defined from this new standpoint: life lived in the expectation of the appearance of this hidden life, of this spiritual life that begins even now. But as yet it is still hidden, and our visible situation might induce us to have doubts about an eternal element in our lives, while all in us recalls death to us and calls us to death. However, the pledge of eternity is present in the Holy Spirit.

> QUESTIONS 106-107. Repeat what remains.—I believe in the resurrection of the body, and the life everlasting.
> Why is this article included in the confession of faith?—To remind us that our happiness is not located on earth. The advantage and use of this knowledge is double. First we are taught that we are to live in this world as foreigners, thinking continually of departure, and not allowing our hearts to be involved in earthly thoughts. Then too, however deeply the fruit of the grace of Christ bestowed upon us may lie hid and buried, we are not therefore to despond, but patiently wait until the day of its revelation.

From time to time we must allow ourselves a small criticism, even of the great Calvin. When Calvin declares that mention of the resurrection of the flesh and of the life everlasting is made so that we may see that our happiness does not lie in earth, of course he is right. But I do not think this negative answer is sufficient or that it is neotestamentary. If Paul had been asked why resurrection of the dead must be spoken of, I think he would have answered: "Now as to us, we are citizens of heaven; and from thence we wait for the Lord Jesus Christ as our Savior, who shall transform our miserable body to make it into the likeness of his glorified body, by his power of subjecting all things unto him." This is more than what Calvin says. For Paul, the acknowledgment that our happiness does not lie in earth is not alone in question. We are enabled furthermore—and primarily—to acknowledge that it lies in heaven, whereto Christ has preceded us, and where he shall transform our miserable body into the image of his glorified body. The resurrection of the flesh therefore implies above all not the scorn of the earth but the love of heaven. Once we have understood that we are snatched by Christ out of the dominion of sin and death, the notion of a strange country, which Calvin speaks of, becomes sensible and comprehensible. The strange country is not the world as such (for in reference to what would it be strange?) but as the place of our remoteness from God. To such a world, we are enabled not to cling. We live in the dark and sinister world where there are so many complaints, miseries and catastrophes. But we know this is not our country. And, already in this world, we can be joyful, our eyes fixed on Holy Zion, the eternal fatherland. We are able to have no fear. We are enabled not to lose courage. We have permission to live. We shall go on our way. One day, it will be death, the end, as they say. But this end is not the end. And all the horrors of this earthly ending cannot convince us that life is vain and that we live a lost life.

QUESTION 108. What, then, will be the order of resurrection?—Those who were dead before will receive their bodies, the same as they had before, but endowed with the new quality of being no longer liable to death and corruption. But those who will then be living, God will marvelously raise up by sudden change (I Cor. 15:52).

For an explanation of resurrection, Calvin re-
sorted to the medieval philosophical difference between substance and quality. Substance is perma-
nent, but qualities may change. Because of the
resurrection, human life does remain the same, but
its qualities have changed. We should read again
and study I Cor. 15, that we may get an idea of
the resurrection, of this absolute change, which
rather than an ending, is a beginning again of life.
Besides, we could not ever imagine for ourselves
these things except with the imperfect means of our
philosophical categories. We have no idea either of
the life beyond or of the passage of this life into the
other. We have only what came to pass in Jesus
Christ, in his reign, which is present with us
through faith, and which is declared to us. What
we dare believe, is that we participate in this
change, in the effects of human sanctification that
occurred in the resurrection of Jesus Christ.

Even though we cannot imagine for ourselves
the resurrection—and we simply cannot—it is important to retain at least this: if resurrection is a
passage, if it endows us with absolutely new qualities, still it deals with this same life, our life that
we live here. It deals with the appearing of eternal
life in our life itself as it is. Often I have tried to
imagine this for myself in this following manner:
our life is hidden under a veil. This veil is the
present times. At the resurrection, this veil will be
removed, and our whole life, from the crib to the
grave, will be seen in the light and in its unity with
the life of Christ, in the splendor of Christ's mercy,
of his grace and of his power. Maybe, there is even
no need for trying to understand the why of these
things: we have only to look to Christ, stop at our

union with him and live in the hope of the un-
veiling, the disclosure, of this our life that will appear in his light.

QUESTION 109. But will it be the same for the pious
and the impious?—There will be a single resurrection for all; but their states will differ (John
5:29; Matt. 25:46). For some will rise to salvation
and bliss; others to death and extreme misery.

The resurrection being the complete disclosure
of our life, all is disclosed: our faith and lack of
faith, our justification and condemnation, all that
grace has done well in us and all that we have not
done well by resisting grace. Each of us shall be
what in reality he is. The resurrection is then the
supreme judgment through which we must enter
into eternal life.

But we may not contemplate resurrection and
judgment independently of Jesus Christ, as though
we were alone before God, as though our faith were
a work we might show forth to God. Therefore it
will be proper to remember here what Calvin—
correcting beforehand the harshness of his Question 109—said in Questions 86-87: "Does it give
any happiness to our conscience to know that
Christ will one day judge the world?—Indeed, a
quite peculiar happiness. For we know that he will
come for our salvation only.—Then it is not proper
that we should dread this judgment as though it
struck terror into us?—No, indeed, since we shall
stand only at the tribunal of a judge who is also
our advocate, and who has taken us into his faithful protection." What will be disclosed is indeed
our condemnation. But it is also our salvation in

Jesus Christ, our judge and our advocate in one person. Participating in the exchange of lives between God and us, we have seen that Jesus Christ has taken on our sin. We contemplate now the other aspect of this exchange: we take on his justice, his holiness; all that is divine in us (and therefore foreign to us) is transferred to us. We are just, holy, good (one hardly dares say so), not with a justice, with a holiness and a goodness that would emanate from our attitudes and our actions, but with a justice, with a holiness and a goodness foreign to and given us. Christ is now the sinner and I am the just one. Upon this exchange I am his property, the object of his vigilance. I am now his concern. He will help me, he will be on my side. He may forsake me. I shall certainly die, all of us will die, but in spite of death we shall be accompanied by him. We shall be judged, but with him. We shall be condemned, but with him. And there lies our salvation. Our Lord himself has declared for his solidarity with us.

Three more remarks on the resurrection.

1. *All is accomplished.* That we may well understand the question of eschatology, we must always tackle it through the fact: all is accomplished. We are the children of God; there is nothing we may become. Actually all is in order. All is good, even as God when the world was created found it "good." We are God's children, we enjoy his goodness and his power, his Covenant with us based upon his union within himself, Father, Son and Holy Spirit. The Christian life begins with thanksgiving and not with distress and despair. One cannot begin with despair

and end up with hope. This does not work! One can but begin with thanksgiving, the child-like absolutely simple joy. Eschatology means the last things. These last things may be tackled only by beginning with the beginning. The beginning is the truth that God so loved the world that he gave his only Son. There is nothing to be added. There is nothing new that would better this real-ity of love—a light wherein we are permitted to live.

2. *We live by faith and not by sight.* We live in the Dominion of Christ. But this Dominion— which embraces our lives—is still veiled. This veil is not only death, sin, catastrophe, wars, it is, more centrally, the contradiction of the Prince of this world to the Lord of the world, which is made manifest in all sorts of particular contra-dictions. There is the spirit and, on the other hand, the flesh, the Spirit of God and the human flesh (that is, the totality of man as such). Paul said so: "If I live in the flesh, I live in the faith in the Son of God." We do know it is the Spirit that is valuable; nevertheless, the flesh continues to exist, this flesh like myself, myself as my own enemy. This contradiction is now ineluctable, and let us hope it is salutary! The grand accom-plished reality is not yet unveiled, not yet dis-closed. It is announced through a movement: the movement manifested in the life of this poor Church and in the life of the world perhaps. There are signs and signs against these signs. There is the truth and contradiction against the truth. We live by faith, but we live by faith always while being sinners and having so many

things, big and little, to reproach ourselves with. We are threatened, all of us, thoroughly, and then we believe, but we believe as such—as being threatened. We have peace. (Cf. Rom. 5:1.) But we have this peace only in full fight. And woe to us if we should want to have peace without the fight. Until our death and until Christ's return and till the end of the world, this war will last on. It will always be difficult to live. One believes he has understood something, one believes he has made some progress. One relapses again, and once again it gets complicated. We live in contradiction. What is it, this life that ends up in the grave, the coffin? One does not like to think about it, does one, about the coffin! One would like to avoid this grave. But we will get there, and that is our life. I remember a very well-known man in the Christian world who confided to me, once in an hour of confidence, "You know, Karl, I don't like to think about death!" I told him, "Neither do I!" One would like to live as the patriarchs of old: three hundred, four hundred, nine hundred years. At last, after nine hundred years, they had to die, and this was perhaps even more serious. No one, I think, could understand the strength and the power of this word "resurrection" if he finds life miserable and simply boring. Only those who love life can understand what it is to lose it and have the assurance that they shall have life and the life everlasting. We want to love life, but we are sure that we shall lose it. Herein lies the contradiction in which we are plunged. There you have what Calvin called the strange country, yes, really strange in all regards.

3. *The solution of the contradiction.* Our situation full of contradictions is not a dualism wherein God might be counterbalanced by evil, life by death, etc. No, it is rather comparable to an object lighted in a certain way, and which later will be lighted in another way. We live in the brightness of Christ's kingdom established even now, but which shall be revealed then. We shall have eyes to see our life "unveiled" and we shall see all reality such as it is. By this light and by this new vision of God, our life shall be transformed. Transformed because unveiled. Transformed while remaining selfsame, transformed because reaching its proper meaning at last.

V. THE LIFE EVERLASTING

Question 110

QUESTION 110. Why, then, is there mention only of external life and not of hell?—Since nothing is held by faith except what contributes to the consolation of the souls of the pious. Hence there are here recalled the rewards which the Lord has prepared for his servants. Therefore it is not added what fate may await the impious whom we know to be outcasts from the Kingdom of God.

For the third time, it is a question of human life under the aspect of the future that is promised to it by God, under the aspect of its eternity. Our life in the light of eternity is the life everlasting. Justified through the forgiveness of sins, sanctified through the resurrection of the flesh, human life is

glorified through the life everlasting. (Cf. Rom. 8.)
The Holy Spirit communicates to us communion
with God not only in justifying us and in sanctify-
ing us, but in glorifying us, that is, in communicat-
ing the glory of God to us. Glory means the splendor of God, the glory of God in the life and the
revelation of God such as he is. God has but to
show himself to make light and to dazzle. (Cf.
Question 2.) Do note that, though it is a question
of glorification, this does not mean that there is a
glory within us that might start to shine, but it
means that we shall partake in a glory other than
ours, in the glory of God. We shall be, so to speak,
draped in his light. We ourselves shall shine because we shall be lighted. God will have his glory
in us and that is the goal of his creation: God does
not want to remain alone. It is not enough for God
to shine by his own power. He wants to shine in
others and he chose us to live in us. He wants to
be glorious in us and through us. The "veil" of
which we spoke will be removed and human life
will meet its final destination visibly.

In the sense of the Bible, the term eternal (αἰώνιος)
does not mean "which has no end," but quite simply: "which belongs in the world to come." Eternity is, in the Bible, the time of this new world.
Hence it is not defined first by its unlimited characteristic (indeed it is unlimited) but by its relation
to the world to come, to the glorious Kingdom of
God.

According to Calvin, the Creed does not speak of
hell and eternal death because its author was nice
enough to be willing to speak only of comfort. But
Calvin, as if to restore things, reminds us that there

is also hell, although the Creed did not mention it.
I think that, here too, Calvin must be slightly cor-
rected. It is not only out of kindness, out of good
nature, that the Creed does not mention hell and
eternal death. But the Creed discusses only the
things which are the object of the faith. We do not
have to believe in hell and in eternal death. I may
only believe in the resurrection and the judgment
of Christ, the judge and advocate, who has loved me
and defended my cause.

The Creed discusses the things to be believed.
To believe. It is important to finish with faith. We
believe in the Word of God and it is the word of
our salvation. The kingdom, the glory, the resurrection, the life everlasting, each one is a work of
rescue. Light pierces through the darkness, eternal
life overcomes eternal death. We cannot "believe"
in sin, in the devil, in our death sentence. We can
only believe in the Christ who has overcome the
devil, borne sin and removed eternal death. Devil,
sin, and eternal death appear to us only when they
are overcome.

And let us not add: "Yes, but sin is a grievous
thing"—as though hell and so many horrors were
not on earth already! If one does really believe, one
cannot say: "But!" this terrible and pitiful "but."
I fear that much of the weakness of our Christian
witness comes from this fact that we dare not
frankly confess the grandeur of God, the victory of
Christ, the superiority of the Spirit. Wretched as
we are, we always relapse into contemplation of
ourselves and of mankind, and, naturally, eternal
death comes up no sooner than we have looked on
it. The world without redemption becomes again

a power and a threatening force, and our message of victory ceases to be believable. But as it is written: "The victory that triumphs over the world, this is our faith (I John 5:4).

BIBLIOGRAPHY

A. BIBLIOGRAPHICAL INFORMATION

Many articles and essays by Barth on various topics pertaining to the beginnings of his theological movement are found in the periodical *Zwischen den Zeiten,* annotated by K. Barth, Ed. Thurneysen and F. Gogarten, and published in Munich from 1923 to 1933.

In 1933 Barth and Thurneysen founded and edited a series of brochures under the title *Theologische Existenz heute.* The series contains sixty-two volumes and was also published in Munich (Chr. Kaiser) from 1933 to 1939.

Since 1938, a similar series, *Theologische Studien,* has been edited by K. Barth and is being published now by the Evangelischer Verlag, in Zollikon, Zuerich.

Theologische Existenz *heute, Neue Folge,* was revived in 1946 under the editorship of K. G. Steck and G. Eichholtz, and is published by Kaiser, Munich. *N.F.* will signify *Neue Folge.*

E.T. means English translation.

B. BIBLIOGRAPHY

Works by Karl Barth

1. *Die Auferstehung der Toten;* Muenchen: Christian Kaiser, 1924; Zollikon—Zuerich: Evangelischer Verlag A.G. 1953, 4th edition. Interpretation of I Corinthians 15. E.T.

2. *"Das Bekenntnis der Reformation und unser Bekennen"; Theologische Existenz heute,* Heft 29, 1935.

3. *"Die Botschaft von der freien Gnade Gottes"; Theologische Studien,* Heft 23, 1947. Ev. Verlag.

4. *"Calvin"; Theologische Existenz heute,* Heft 37, 1936.

5. *"Calvinfeier 1936"; Theologische Existenz heute,* Heft 43, 1936.

6. "Preface" to *Calvin* (a selection by Ch. Gagnebin), Paris: L.U.F.—Egloff, 1948.

7. *"Der Christ als Zeuge"; Theologische Existenz heute,* Heft 12, 1934. E.T. in *God in Action.*

8. *"Christengemeinde und Buergergemeinde"; Theologische Studien,* Heft 20, 1946. E.T. in *Against the Stream.*

9. *The Christian Churches and Living Reality;* translated by E. Allan, London: Hutchinson, 1946.

10. *Die christliche Gemeinde im Wechselder Staatsordnungen;* Dokumente einer Ungarnreise Zollikon-Zuerich: Evangelischer Verlag A.G., 1948. Report on a trip to Hungary. E.T. in *Against the Stream.*

11. *Die christliche Lehre nach dem Heidelberger Katechismus;* Zollikon-Zuerich: Evangelischer Verlag A.G., 1948.

12. *Vom christlichen Leben;* Muenchen: Christian Kaiser, 1926; 2nd edition, 1928. E.T.

13. *Die christliche Verkuendigung im heutigen Europa;* Muenchen: C. Kaiser, 1946. Pamphlet. E.T. in *Against the Stream.*
14. "*Das christliche Verstaendnis der Offenbarung*"; *Theologische Existenz heute, Neue Folge,* Heft 12, 1948 E.T. in *Against the Stream.*
15. "*Christus und Adam nach Roemer*" 5; *Theologische Studien,* Heft 35, 1952. E.T.
16. *Christus und wir Christen;* Zollikon-Zuerich: Evangelischer Verlag A.G., 1947, *Theologische Existenz heute, Neue Folge,* Heft 11, Muenchen: Christian Kaiser, 1947.
17. "The Church—The living Congregation of the living Lord Jesus Christ"; Man's Disorder and God's Design (Amsterdam Assembly of the World Council of Churches), New York: Harper, 1949, published partially in the *Christian Century,* December 8, 1948, under the title "No Christian Marshall Plan!" See also: Reinhold Niebuhr: "We are Men not God," *Christian Century,* October 27, 1948; Karl Barth: "Continental vs Anglo-Saxon Theology," *Ibid.* February 16, 1949; R. Niebuhr: "An Answer to Karl Barth," *Ibid.* February 23, 1949.
18. *La Confession de Foi de l'Eglise,* Neuchâtel: Delachaux & Niestlé, 1943. E.T.
19. *Credo;* Muenchen: Christian Kaiser 1935: Zollikon-Zuerich: Evangelischer Verlag A.G., 1948.
20. "*David Friedrich Strauss als Theologe*"; *Theologische Studien,* Heft 6, 1939.
21. *Die Deutshen und Wir;* Zollikon-Zuerich: Evangelischer Verlag A.G., 1945.
22. "*Der Dienst am Wort Gottes*"; *Theologische Existenz heute,* Heft 13, 1934. E.T. in *God in Action.*
23. "*Dietrich Bonhoeffer und Karl Barth*" (Ein Briefwechsel aus den Jahren 1933-1934), *Evangelische Theologie* 1955, Heft 4-5, Muenchen: Christian Kaiser, 1955. Cited in *Antwort.*

24. *Dogmatik im Grundriss;* Zollikon-Zuerich: Evangelischer Verlag A.G., 1947. E.T.

25. *Erklaerung des Philipperbriefes;* Zollikon-Zuerich: Evangelischer Verlag A.G., 1947, 5th edition. First published in 1928.

26. *"Das Evangelium in der Gegenwart"; Theologische Existenz heute,* Heft 25, 1935.

27. *"Evangelium und Bildung"; Theologische Studien,* Heft 2, 1938.

28. *"Evangelium und Gesetz"; Theologische Existenz heute,* Heft 32, 1935. Second edition 1956, *Neue Folge,* Heft 50.

29. *Fides quaerens intellectum;* Anselms Beweis der Existenz Gottes, Muenchen: Christian Kaiser, 1931.

30. *"Die Frage nach der Taufe"; Evangelische Theologie* 1949-1950, Heft 4. Cited in *Antwort.* E.T.

31. *"Fuer die Freiheit des Evangeliums"; Theologische Existenz heute,* Heft 2, 1933.

32. *"Das Geschenk der Freiheit"; Theologische Studien,* Heft 39.

33. *Gespraeche nach Amsterdam;* (J. Danielou, R. Niebuhr, K. Barth). Zollikon-Zuerich: Evangelischer Verlag A.G. 1949. *"Amsterdamer Fragen und Antworten"; Theologische Existenz heute, Neue, Folge,* Heft 15, 1949.

34. *"Gottes Gnadenwahl"; Theologische Existenz heute,* Heft 47, 1936.

35. *"Gottes Wille und unsere Wuensche"; Theologische Existenz heute,* Heft 7, 1934.

36. *"Der Gute Hirte"; Theologische Existenz heute,* Heft 10, 1934.

37. "How my mind has changed"; *Christian Century,* September 13 and 20, 1939.

38. "How my mind has changed, 1938-1949"; *Christian Century,* March 9, 1949.

39. *"Humanismus"; Theologische Studien,* Heft 28, 1950.

40. *Karfreitag und Ostern* (with E. Thurneysen), Basel: Evangelische Buchhandlung, 1943.

41. *Kerygma und Mythos;* vol. II, ed. by H. W. Bartsch, Hamburg: H. Reich, 1952.

42. *"Die Kirche Jesu Christi"; Theologische Existenz heute,* Heft 5, 1933.

43. *"Die Kirche und die Kirchen"; Theologische Existenz heute,* Heft 27, 1935. E.T.

44. *Die Kirche zwischen Ost und West;* Zollikon-Zuerich: Evangelischer Verlag A.G., 1949. Brochure. Replied to by E. G. Rusch: *Die Kirche zwischen Ost und West: Lavaters Antwort an Karl Barth.* St. Gallen: Vadian-Verlag, 1949. E.T. in *Against the Stream.*

45. *Die kirchliche Dogmatik I; Die Lehre vom Worte Gottes,* 1, Muenchen: Christian Kaiser, 1932. Zollikon-Zeurich: Evangelischer Verlag, 1952, 6th edition; 1955, 7th edition. E.T.

46. *Die kirchliche Dogmatik I; Die Lehre vom Worte Gottes,* 2. Zollikon-Zuerich: Evangelischer Verlag A.G., 1948, 4th edition; Zollikon: Evangelische Buchhandlung, 1938. E.T.

47. *Die kirchliche Dogmatik II; Die Lehre von Gott,* 1. Zollikon-Zuerich: Evangelischer Verlag A.G., 1948.

48. *Die kirchliche Dogmatik II; Die Lehre von Gott,* 2. Zollikon-Zuerich: Evangelischer Verlag A.G., 1942. E.T.

49. *Die kirchliche Dogmatik III; Die Lehre von der Schoepfung,* 1. Zollikon-Zuerich: Evangelischer Verlag A.G., 1945.

50. *Die kirchliche Dogmatik III; Die Lehre von der Schoepfung,* 2. Zollikon-Zuerich: Evangelischer Verlag A.G., 1948.

51. *Die kirchliche Dogmatik III; Die Lehre von der Schoepfung,* 3. Zollikon-Zuerich: Evangelischer Verlag A.G., 1950.

52. *Die kirchliche Dogmatik III; Die Lehre von der*

Schoepfung, 4 (Ethics). Zollikon-Zuerich: Evangelischer Verlag A.G., 1951.

53. *Die kirchliche Dogmatik IV; Die Lehre von der Versoehnung,* 1. Zollikon-Zuerich: Evangelischer Verlag A.G., 1953.

54. *Die kirchliche Dogmatik IV; Die Lehre von der Versoehnung,* 2. Zollikon-Zuerich: Evangelischer Verlag A.G., 1955.

55. *"Die kirchliche Lehre von der Taufe"; Theologische Studien,* Heft 14, 1943. *Theologische Existenz heute, N.F.,* Heft 4, 1947.

56. *The Knowledge of God and the Service of God;* according to the teaching of the Reformation. Gifford Lectures, 1937-1938, translated by J. L. M. Haire and Ian Henderson. London: Hodder & Stoughton, 1938. Based on the Scottish Confession of 1560.

57. *"Die lebendige Gemeinde und die freie Gnade"; Theologische Existenz heute, Neue Folge,* Heft 9, 1947.

58. *Die Lehre vom Worte Gottes; Prolegomena zur christlichen Dogmatik,* Muenchen: Christian Kaiser, 1927. The first edition of K.B.'s Prolegomena to his *Dogmatik,* later significantly re-titled *Dogmatik.*

59. *"A letter to American Christians"; Christendom,* vol. 8, no. 4, 1943.

60. *A letter to Great Britain from Switzerland;* London: The Sheldon Press, 1941. Published in the U.S. under the title *This Christian Cause;* N.Y.: Macmillan, 1941. Two letters to the French Protestants and A Letter to Great Britain. On religion and the war.

61. *"Lutherfeier 1933"; Theologische Existenz heute,* Heft 4, 1933.

62. *"Nein! Antwort an Emil Brunner"; Theologische Existenz heute,* Heft 14, 1934. K.B.'s controversial

refutation of Brunner's vindication of general revelation.

63. *Not und Verheissung im deutschen Kirchenkampf;* Bern: BEG-Verlag, 1938. Pamphlet. E.T.

64. *Die oekumenische Aufgabe in den reformierten Kirchen der Schweiz;* Zollikon-Zuerich: Evangelischer Verlag A.G., 1949. With contributions by E. Brunner and E. Studer.

65. *"Offenbarung, Kirche, Theologie"; Theologische Existenz heute,* Heft 9, 1934. E.T. in *God in Action.*

66. *"Politische Entscheidung in der Einheit des Glaubens"; Theologische Existenz heute, N.F.,* Heft 34, 1952. E.T. in *Against the Stream.*

67. *La Prière;* Neuchâtel and Paris: Delachaux & Niestlé, 1949. According to the catechisms of the Reformation on the Lord's Prayer. E.T.

68. *"Das Problem der Ethik in der Gegenwart; Zwischen den Zeiten,* Heft 2, 30-57, 1923.

69. "Protestant Churches in Europe"; *Foreign Affairs,* January, 1943.

70. *Die Protestantische Theologie im 19. Jahrhundert; Ihre Vorgeschichte und Geschichte;* Zollikon-Zuerich: Evangelischer Verlag A.G., 1947. Contains also illuminating reappraisals of Rousseau and Hegel.

71. *"Protestantismus der Gegenwart: Jugend und Krisis der Kultur," Internationale Zeitschrift fuer Kultur und Kunst,* 1932. Cited in *Antwort.*

72. *"Rechtfertigung und Recht"; Theologische Studien,* Heft 1, Zollikon: Evangelische Buchhandlung, 1938. 2nd edition, Zollikon-Zuerich: Ev. Verlag A.G., 1944. E.T.

73. *"Reformation als Entscheidung"; Theologische Existenz heute,* Heft 3, 1933.

74. *Revelation;* London: Faber and Faber, 1937. Cited in *Antwort.*

75. *Der Roemerbrief;* Bern: G. A. Baeschlin, 1919; Muenchen: Christian Kaiser, 1920; 2nd edition (revised), 1922; Zollikon-Zuerich: Evangelischer Verlag A.G., 1954. This book theologically divides the 19th century from the 20th. E.T.

76. *"Der roemische Katholizismus als Frage an die Protestantische Kirche," Zwischen den Zeiten,* IV, Muenchen: Christian Kaiser, 1928.

77. *"Rudolph Bultmann: ein Versuch ihn zu verstehen"; Theologische Studien,* Heft 34, 1952.

78. *"Die Schrift und die Kirche"; Theologische Studien,* Heft 22, 1947.

79. *"Die Souveraenitaet des Worte Gottes und die Entscheidung des Glaubens"; Theologische Studien,* Heft 5, 1939.

80. *Eine Schweizer Stimme 1938-1945;* Zollikon-Zuerich: Evangelischer Verlag A.G., 1945. Selected essays. Partially translated.

81. *Die Theologie und die Kirche;* Muenchen: Christian Kaiser, 1928. On Lord's Supper, Reformed Churches, Schleiermacher and his School, Roman Catholicism. Contains *"Frage an das Christentum,"* E.T., "Questions to Christendom."

82. *"Theologie und die Mission in der Gegenwart"; Zwischen den Zeiten* X, 189-215, 1932.

83. *"Theologische Existenz heute"; Theologische Existenz heute,* Heft 1, 8th edition. Muenchen: Christian Kaiser, 1933. Originally published in *Zwischen den Zeiten.*

84. *Die Unordnung der Welt und Gottes Heilsplan;* Zollikon-Zuerich: Ev. Verlag, 1948.

85. *Weihnacht;* Muenchen: Ch. Kaiser, 1934. Sermons.

86. *Wie Koennen die Deutschen gesund werden;* Zollikon-Zuerich: Ev. Verlag A.G., 1945.

87. *"Die Wirklichkeit des neuen Menschen"; Theologische Studien,* Heft 27.

88. *Wolfgang Amadeus Mozart;* Zollikon-Zuerich: 1956.

89. *Das Wort Gottes und die Theologie;* Muenchen: Christian Kaiser, 1924, 1925.
90. *"Zwei Vortraege"; Theologische Existenz,* N.F., Heft 3, 1946. On Christian ethics.
91. *"Die Menschlichkeit Gottes"; Theologische Studien,* Heft 48, 1957.
92. *"Evangelische Theologie im 19. Jahrhundert"; Theologische Studien,* Heft 49, 1957.

C. WORKS BY KARL BARTH IN ENGLISH TRANSLATION
(*See also* 9, 17, 37, 56, 59, 60, 74.)

Against the Stream (short post-war writings, 1946-1952). Translated by E. M. Delacour and St. Godman; edited by R. G. Smith. London: Student Christian Movement Press, 1954. E.T. of 10, 13, 14, 44, 66, and essays on Humanism, Poverty, Revelation, the Jewish question.

Christ and Adam: Man and Humanity in Romans 5. Translated by T. A. Smail. New York: Harper, 1957. Introduction by W. Pauck. E.T. of 15.

The Christian Life. Translated by J. Strathearn McNab. London: Student Christian Movement Press, 1930; Hodder & Stoughton, 1935. E.T. of 12.

The Church and the Churches, Grand Rapids, Mich.: Wm. B. Eardmans, 1936. A message to the World Conference on Faith and Order, Edinburgh, 1937. E.T. of 43.

The Church and the Political Problem of Our Day, London: Hodder & Stoughton; New York: Scribners, 1939. E.T. of 80.

Church and State. Translated by G. Ronald Howe. London: Student Christian Movement Press, 1939. E.T. of 72.

The Church and the War. Translated by A. H. Froendt; introduction by Samuel McCrea Cavert.

New York: Macmillan, 1944. E.T. of 80. A letter to the French Protestants.

Church Dogmatics I: The Doctrine of the Word of God, Part 1. Translated by G. T. Thomson. Edinburgh: T. & T. Clark, 1936. E.T. of 45.

Church Dogmatics I: The Doctrine of the Word of God, Part 2. G. W. Bromiley and T. F. Torrance, general editors. Edinburgh: T. & T. Clark, 1956. E.T. of 46.

Church Dogmatics II: The Doctrine of God, Part 1, Edinburgh: T. & T. Clark, 1957. E.T. of 47.

Church Dogmatics II: The Doctrine of God, Part 2, Edinburgh: T. &. T. Clark, 1957. E.T. of 48.

Church Dogmatics IV: The Doctrine of Reconciliation, Part 1, Edinburgh: T. & T. Clark, 1956. E.T. of 53.

Come Holy Spirit. Sermons by K. Barth and Ed. Thurneysen. Translated by G. W. Richards, E. G. Homrighausen and K. J. Ernst. New York: Round Table Press, 1934.

Credo. Translated by Strathearn McNab. London: Hodder & Stoughton, 1936. The Chief Problems of Dogmatics with reference to the Apostle's Creed; lectures delivered at the University of Utrecht in 1935. E.T. of 19.

Dogmatics in Outline. Translated by G. T. Thamson. New York: Philosophical Library, 1949. A presentation of Christian Doctrine based on the Apostle's Creed. E.T. of 24.

The Epistle to the Romans. Translated by Edwyn C. Hoskyns. London: Oxford University Press, 1933. With a new preface by the author. E.T. of 75.

The Faith of the Church. Translated by G. Vahanian. New York; Meridian Books, 1958. E.T. of 18.

"Feuerbach—An Introductory Essay" (translated by J. L. Adams) in L. Feuerbach, The Essence of Christianity, New York: Harper Torchbooks, 1957.

The Germans and Ourselves. Translated by R. G. Smith. London: Nisbet & Company, 1945. With an introduction by A. R. Vidler. E.T. of 21.

God in Action. Translated by G. W. Richards, E. G. Homrighausen, K. J. Ernst. New York: Round Table Press, 1936. E.T. of 7, 22, 65.

God's Search for Man. Translated by G. W. Richards, E. G. Homrighausen, K. J. Ernst. New York: Round Table Press, 1935. E.T. of *Die grosse Barmherzigkeit.* Sermons of K. Barth and Ed. Thurneysen.

The Holy Ghost and the Christian Life. Translated by R. Birch Hoyle. London: F. Muller, 1938.

Natural Theology, comprising "Nature and Grace" by E. Brunner and the reply "No!" by K. Barth. Translated by P. Fraenkel, with an introduction by John Baillie. London: Geoffrey Bles, Centenary Press, 1946. E.T. of 62.

"The New Humanism and the Humanism of God." Translated by F. Herzog. *Theology Today,* July 1951. E.T. of K. Barth's address to the Rencontres Internationales, Geneva, 1949. Another translation in *Against the Stream.*

The Only Way: How can the Germans be cured? (Contents: How can the Germans be cured? translated by M. K. Neufeld; The Germans and ourselves, translated by R. G. Smith). New York: Philosophical Library, 1947. E.T. of 21 and 86.

Prayer. Translated by Sara F. Terrien. Philadelphia: Westminster Press, 1950. E.T. of 68.

Questions to Christendom. Translated by Birch Hoyle. London: The Lutterworth Press, 1932. E.T. of 80.

The Resurrection of the Dead. Translated by H. J. Stenning. London: Hodder & Stoughton, 1933. E.T. of 1.

The Teaching of the Church regarding Baptism. Translated by E. A. Payne. London: Student Christian Movement Press, 1948. E.T. of 30.

Theological Existence Today (A plea for theological freedom). Translated by R. Birch Hoyle. London: Hodder & Stoughton, 1933. E.T. of 83.

Trouble and Promise in the Struggle of the Church in Germany. Translated by P. V. M. Benecke. Oxford: Clarendon Press, 1938. Also under the title *The German Church Struggle: tribulation and promise.* London, 1938. E.T. of 63.

The Word of God and the Word of Man. Translated by Douglas Horton. Boston: The Pilgrim Press, 1928; New York: Harper Torchbooks, 1957. E.T. of 89.

D. CONCERNING THE THEOLOGY OF KARL BARTH

Antwort: Karl Barth zum 70. Geburtstag am 10. Mai 1956; Zollikon-Zuerich: Evangelischer Verlag A.G., 1956. A *Festschrift* including Christians and non-Christians.

E. L. Allen: *A guide to the thought of Karl Barth;* the sovereignty of God and the word of God. London: Hodder & Stoughton, n.d.

P. Althaus: *Was ist die Taufe?* Goettingen: Vandenhoeck & Ruprecht, 1950.

K. Ballmer: *Ein Schweizerischer Staatsrechtlehrer;* Melide (Switzerland): 1941.

H. U. von Balthasar: *Karl Barth; Darstellung und Deutung einer Theologie;* Koeln: J. Hegner, 1951. A Roman Catholic who loves St. Thomas and K. Barth.

G. C. Berkouwer: *The Triumph of Grace in the Theology of Karl Barth;* (Translated by H. R. Boer); Grand Rapids, Mich.: Wm. B. Eerdmans, 1956.

H. Bouillard: *Karl Barth,* 3 vols.; Paris Aubier, 1957. Birth and growth of "Neo-Orthodoxy." The Word of God and the meaning of human existence.

E. Buess: *Zur Praedertinationslehre Karl Barths;* Theologische Studien, Heft 43, Zollikon-Zuerich: Evangelischer Verlag, 1955.

F. W. Camfield, ed., *Reformation old and new* (a tribute to Karl Barth). London: Lutterworth Press, 1947.

H. Diem: *Karl Barths Kritik und deutschen Luthertum;* Zollikon-Zuerich: Evangelischer Verlag, 1947.

A. M. Fairweather: *The Word as Truth;* a critical examination of the Christian doctrine in the writings of Thomas Aquinas and Karl Barth. London: Lutterworth Press, 1944.

Heinrich Fries: *Bultmann, Barth und die katholische Theologie;* Stuttgart: Schwabenverlag, 1955.

B. Gherardini: *La parola di Dio nella theologia di Karl Barth;* Rome: Editrice Studium, 1955.

F. Gogarten: *Gericht oder Skepsis: eine Streitschrift gegen Karl Barth;* Jena: Diederich, 1937. A former friend of Barth.

F. Gruenagel, ed.: *Was ist Taufe? Eine Auseinandersetzung mit Karl Barth.* Stuttgart: Evangelisches Verlagswerk, 1951.

Festgabe fuer Karl Barth zum 70. Geburtstag; (Theologische Zeitschrift, 2 vols.). Basel: Fr. Reinhardt A.G.

J. Hamer: *L'occasionalisme théologique de Karl Barth; étude sur sa méthode dogmatique.* Paris: Desclée de Brouwer, 1949. A Roman Catholic negative evaluation.

Hommage et Reconnaissance. Neuchâtel and Paris: Delachaux et Niestlé, 1946. For K. B.'s 60th birthday.

P. Lehmann: "Barth and Brunner: The Dilemma of the Protestant Mind," *Journal of Religion,* April 1940.

P. Lehmann: *Forgiveness;* decisive issue in Protestant thought (Foreword by Reinhold Niebuhr). New York: Harper & Brothers, 1940.

H. R. Machintosh: *Types of Modern Theology.* London: Nisbet, 1937. From Schleiermacher to Barth.

S. Navarria: *Sören Kierkegaard e l'irrazionalismo di Karl Barth.* Palermo: Palumbo, 1943.

T. H. L. Parker, ed: *Essays in Christology for Karl Barth.* London: Lutterworth Press, 1956.

W. Pauck: *Karl Barth, prophet of a new Christianity?* 1931.

W. C. Robinson: "An Interview with Professor Karl Barth"; Columbia Theological Seminary Bulletin, November 1938.

Julius Schniewind: *Entmythologisierung; eine Auseinandersetzung zwischen J. Schniewind, R. Bultmann und K. Barth.* Stuttgart: Evangelischer Verlagswerk, 1949.

Theology Today: "Articles in Honor of Karl Barth." *Theology Today,* Vol. 13, no. 3, October 1956.

Theologische Aufsaetze; Karl Barth zum 50. Geburtstag. Muenchen: Christian Kaiser, 1936.

J. H. Thomas: "Christology of Sören Kierkegaard and Karl Barth." *Hibbert Journal,* April 1955.

C. van Til: "Has Karl Barth become orthodox?" *Westminster Theological Journal,* May 1954.

C. van Til: *The New Modernism;* an appraisal of the Theology of Barth and Brunner. Philadelphia: Presbyterian and Reformed Publishing Company, 1946. A view from Protestant Orthodoxy.

Otto Weber: *Karl Barth's Church Dogmatics;* an introductory report on vol. I, 1 to III, 4. Translated by A. C. Cochrane. Philadelphia: Westminster, 1953. A faithful and ingenious summary.

Otto Weber, W. Kreck, E. Wolff: *Die Predigt von der Gnadenwahl; Karl Barth zum 10. Mai 1951. Theologische Existenz heute,* N.F., 28.

D. D. Williams: "Brunner and Barth on Philosophy," *Journal of Religion,* October 1947.

LIVING AGE BOOKS

Published by MERIDIAN BOOKS INC.
17 Union Square West, New York 3, New York

LIVING AGE BOOKS, an inexpensive paperbound series, contains works of proven merit on history, art, literature, theology and Biblical studies, as they illuminate the development of Christian tradition in the West.

Titles listed here are not necessarily available in the British Empire.

MERIDIAN BOOKS

17 Union Square West, New York 3, New York

Titles listed here are not necessarily available in the British Empire.

Titles listed here are not necessarily available in the British Empire.